Praise for Branded

"Quart is brilliant."   —*Publishers Weekly* (starred review)

"Fascinating, highly readable cultural study."   *New York Post*

"This book deserves to command wide attention among millions of families."   —*New York Times*

"A fascinating and provocative study."   —*BookPage*

"*Branded* is a cogent wake-up call." —*Los Angeles TimesBook Review*

"This disturbing expose reads like a fantastic horror story—a cross between *Invasion of the Body Snatchers* and *Village of the Damned* — but alas it's true: the author has done her homework, garnered the facts and written them up in a clear, powerful style. We are all in Alissa Quart's debt." —Phillip Lopate, author, *Portrait of My Body*

"*Branded* offers a chilling portrait of the commodification of youth and the innovative ways in which kids resist. Quart's analysis of the intrusion, co-optation and commercialization of young people is a must-read for parents, youth activists, educators, and teenagers alike."   —Donna Gaines, Ph.D., author,
Teenage Wasteland: Suburbia's Dead End Kids

"An excellent book...*Branded* reveals... the way in which young adolescents are being exploited by advertisers, the media and the companies that create products for this age group. Hopefully it will be a heads up for parents, schools, and government agencies to exercise some moral, if not legal, pressure on these institutions to use some restraint and common sense when marketing to young people."   —David Elkind, Ph.D., author
The Hurried Child and *All Grown Up and No Place to Go*

"Alissa Quart takes teenagers seriously, an all too rare and radical thing. While unsparingly exposing adult exploitation of their vulnerability for the market, she manages to keep real kids' strengths center stage. That she lucidly proves her case, detail by disturbing detail, only further shows her own powerful gifts. Read this book."
—Adrian Nicole LeBlanc, author of
*Random Family: Love, Drugs, Trouble,
and Coming of Age in the Bronx*

Photo by Anne Schlechter

About the Author

Alissa Quart is a graduate of Brown University and the Columbia School of Journalism. She has written for publications including *The New York Times, Film Comment, Elle, The Nation, Salon,* and *The Independent* (London). *Branded* is her first book. She lives in New York City.

branded

branded

The Buying and Selling of Teenagers

ALISSA QUART

BASIC
BOOKS

A Member of the Perseus Books Group
New York

Library of Congress Control Number: 2002112393

ISBN 0–7382–0664–4 (hc)   ISBN 0-7382-0862-0 (pbk)

Text design by Trish Wilkinson
Set in 11-point Galliard by the Perseus Books Group

First Edition
  6 7 8 9 10 11 12 13 14 15—07 06 05

to the teenagers who starred in my own adolescence

Contents

Acknowledgments

Thanks to David M. Friedman, Eleana Kim, Jared Hohlt, Mike Scharf, Stuart Lewis, Dan Ferrara, Gerald Burstyn, and Ann Peters for their judicious help in completing this volume. I am also grateful to Nathaniel Wice for all his years of encouragement, as well as my mom, Barbara Koenig Quart, one of the best editors I know, and Matt Hoffman, Rachel Urkowitz, and Kat McGowan for their combined decades worth of support. I am indebted also to my editor, Marnie Cochran, for her care and good sense, and my agent, Peter McGuigan, for his tireless efforts on the book's behalf. Thanks goes to Rachel Heiman, Terry Williams, Nicole Barrett, Owen Gleiberman, Natalie Reitano, and Gavin Smith for productive conversations. Last, I'd like to thank Vic Leviatin and Andrew Courtney of the WISE program, as well as all the teachers and other intermediaries to the land of teen and tween; and, of course, most important, the teens who have shared their stories with me.

Introduction

I WAS ELEVEN YEARS OLD WHEN I HAD MY FIRST BRUSH WITH BRAND consciousness. It was 1983. I played basketball, but terribly. I feared we would all die in our sleep in a rose-hued nuclear winter. I loved Blondie's song "Heart of Glass." I thought I was transparent and breakable like a heart of glass but also secretly cool, like Debbie Harry.

I remember standing in a changing room at Macy's, trying to figure out how to let my inner coolness out. Would Jordache jeans or Esprit corduroys help me? Given my limited allowance (not enough to afford the matching shirt), I knew I would never be mistaken for one of the normal girls in my class. Those girls had shiny hair and perfect Gloria Vanderbilt jeans with white swans embroidered on the back pockets. I attempted to explain the sportswear semiotics to my mother, an earthy feminist, and she responded with solicitous confusion. Why were all these pricey things so necessary? she wondered. Why was normality important? The answer, of course, was simple: The Jordache Look!

Although I didn't know it, I was branding myself for the first time in that changing room, as an Esprit girl. After this moment, I would always be aware that people's clothes and their labels *meant* something about them and that my clothes and their labels meant

something about me. For the next two years, I would still try to resemble the "perfect" girls in my class, those who had pretty hand-
writing. I would also aspire to be like those girls who disco-danced
and shimmied in the television ads for designer jeans. In other words,
I was entering the world of the self-loathing, branded adolescent.

It was not a new terrain. The marketing of products to teenagers,
as a group separate from adults and children, has existed since the
word *teenager* was coined by Madison Avenue in 1941. But there has
been a change in the degree to which young lives are commercial-
ized. The effects of branding on teens and preteens are far worse
than my own miserable dressing-room encounter with the logo almost twenty years ago.

Over the last decade, there has been an exponential increase in
the intensity that manufacturers employ to sell their stuff to the
young. Today's teens are victims of the contemporary luxury economy. They have grown up in the age of the brand, bombarded and
defined by name products and intrusive and clever advertising
strategies. Raised by a commodity culture from the cradle, teens
dependably fragile self-images and their need to belong to groups
are perfect qualities for advertisers to exploit. In *Branded,* I account
for the degree to which teens now consider marketing and promotion in their lives, as buyers of goods and as kids who consider their
own characters and personae brands unto themselves. Kids are
forced to embrace the instrumental logic of consumerism at an ear-
lier-than-ever age. When they visit cities, middle-school students
routinely rush to visit Niketowns, where they snap up the newest
Nike sneakers like aliens returning to the mothership. Girls develop
anorexic behaviors at a younger age than ever before, and advertisements for fast food become more adept at attracting an increasingly
obese child population. "There will be a first step, a first word and,
of course, a first French fry," says a recent McDonald's ad, which
arrives at a time when one-third of American children ages four to

twelve are overweight, an ad that raised hackles among adult protestors when the fast food corporation launched a whole slew of other spots featuring tots, knowing full well that kids now begin asking for brands as soon as they can talk.

These and other developments have had profound and negative consequences on Generation Y, those born between 1979 and 1995. They dream in Hi-definition and Sony sound. Their signs and wonders are the bright logos that line the avenues and shopping malls. Although as a society at large we are inundated by marketing, consuming and finding self-definition in logos and products, teens are the most troubling case study. U.S. teens spent $155 billion in "discretionary income" in 2000 alone, buying clothing, CDs, and makeup.

But companies in 2002 are not only attracted to teens and preteens spending money today, hooking them into a cycle of labor and shopping during their youths. Teen-oriented brands now aim to register so strongly in kids' minds that the appeal will remain for life. Unlike older members of the population, today's teens start life with Disney and Baby Gap, then enter an adolescence of watching Disney-owned Dimension Film horror movies and wearing the Gap company's sub-brand, Old Navy.

Teens suffer more than any other sector of society for this wall-to-wall selling. They are at least as anxious as their parents about having enough money and maintaining their social class, a fear that they have been taught is best allayed by *more* branded gear. And they have taken to branding themselves, believing that the only way to participate in the world is to turn oneself into a corporate product or a corporate spy to help promote the products to other kids.

A counter to the unbearable commercialization of youth arises when teens fight back with an "unbranding" agenda. Some teens begin to suspect advertisers' attempts to seduce them and, when this happens, they see through the smart and chic images of such brands as Starbucks—which, after all, was one of the main targets of the young activists at the 1999 anti–World Trade Organization rally in Seattle. Teenagers are increasingly fighting against the sponsorship of schools and universities. They subvertize, messing with ad slogans to create their own humorously deconstructed versions, such as Starf***s. The success of free software movements, including Linux and music-sharing sites such as Napster, reveals a subversive, communal impulse, as do various Do It Yourself scenes in which teens attempt to make their own cheap or free entertainments to entertain one another.

Inspired by the commercialization of youth and also by the signs of resistance to it, I decided to write *Branded*. The term *brand* suggests both the ubiquity of logos in today's teen dreams and the extreme way these names now define teen identities. My hope is that these stories of kid branding will help to increase understanding of the dangerous consequences of our current materialism.

PART ONE
branding

1

Branded

Coming of age in the 1980s, I was aware of status signs and corporate logos and the distinction between them. I knew that Beatrice owned Tropicana (thanks to the chipper synergic advertising jingle tagline of the period "By Beatrice!"), that when I wore Converse high tops and listened to Joy Division I was branding myself, putting myself on the art punk nostalgic "college rock" side of adolescent style. I considered myself in a style war against the "normal" girls, who wore ZaZu-colored hair and blue jelly shoes, their Polo by Ralph Lauren logos standing proud and emblematic on their cotton shirts. Of course, being a girl whose identity arose from her lack of brands, I had to make sure that everyone knew I was destroying all the logos in my wake. I carefully scissored the labels off my Levi's and Guess jeans. I believed the shadowy tell-tale rectangles and triangles that remained were an aesthetic of renunciation that would speak for me.

Adolescence has been transformed radically since then. No longer can teens' interest in brands be reduced to an ordinary concern with differentiation, or to distinguishing one's identity from that of the group and the converse, that of conforming, or fitting in with the group. The reliance on brands has shifted: brands have in-filtrated preteens and adolescents' inner lives.

You can see the commercial remaking of teenagers in the ads for investment services and credit card companies directed at teens in the high-gloss teen magazines. The companies feign ignorance about the rising rates of credit card debt among the very young, that those under twenty-five are now the fastest-growing group fil-ing for bankruptcy. In blatant disregard for youth consumer debt, financial-services companies now create teenage-oriented credit and cash cards. Among these cards are Visa's Visa Buxx card and the Coca-Cola-owned RocketCash debit card, where parents or other adults can put cash onto a teen's RocketCash account through an advance from the parents' own credit card.

Marketers have expanded their purview to nine-to-thirteen-year-olds as well, rather like urban realtors set on gentrifying neglected neighborhoods. Teen marketers and product managers have ex-panded into this "tween" niche by prepping the kids to be the sort of teen consumers that companies wish for. Companies ranging from Eastman Kodak to the WB channel now explicitly target these child-ish attentions, and car manufacturers angle for them in the hopes that kids will nag their parents for SUVs. It's an important strategy for Radio Disney, which has gathered an audience of 2.2 million kids aged from six to eleven, sitting ducklings for on-air advertisements. As Radio Disney's brand manager crowed, 55 percent of the sta-tion's listening occurs in cars when mom and kid are together: "You get the gatekeeper and the 'nagger' together."

Tweens and younger teens are now the audience for the teen magazines that have also emerged in the last six years, a new wel-ter of high-rolling ventures such as *Teen People, Teen Vogue,* and *Elle Girl.* These, the training wheels of the glossies, prepare girls and boys for the day when they will move on to *People, Vogue,* and *Elle.* The child-age target market makes these magazines' contents all the more alarming. In the 1980s, teen magazines "indicate[d] no uncompromising commitment to the latest fashion. Instead, the emphasis [was] on 'budget buys.' Good value, economy and ideas," as youth theorist Angela McRobbie wrote of the now-defunct British girls' magazine *Jackie*. McRobbie continues, "Similarly, its beauty features tend[ed] to deal with down-market classic images rather than high-fashion beauty styles." The teen mags of my youth, such as *Seventeen*, were full of clumsy fashion spreads featuring down-market items. The lessons of beauty—the teen girl's realm of self-improvement—were cheap and cheerful and had no high-end, expensive brands attached. Today's teen magazines must have celebrities on their covers, one month Jennifer Lopez, the next James King. The magazines now all push pricey clothes, such as the costumery of Stuart Weitzman, Christian Dior, and DKNY. *Teen Vogue* details the costly label-fixated clothing tastes of the stars: Liv Tyler in a Jane Mayle dress, Keith Richards's teen daughter in Frankie B. jeans, Scarlet Johansson squeezed into a "Technicolor Dolce" dress (in deference to the brand Dolce & Gabbana). These magazines construct an unaffordable but palpable world of yearning for girls. We are all too familiar with the negative effects of the model body on girls' self images, but these new magazines do something new: They help to solidify feelings of economic and taste inadequacy in girls. By introducing very young teens to female celebrity and the dressmakers who help create it, these magazines underline that girls are not complete or competitive if they don't wear label dresses at their junior high school dances.

These new teen magazines emerged in the late 1990s, at the same period as the new magalog genre, which crosses magazines with catalogues (the catalog for the clothing company Delia*s is a classic magalog, full of wistful, poetic copy about love and freedom that loops around outfits, sizes, and prices.) The teen magazines themselves are informal catalogues, and, like adult magazines, they often cross the line between editorializing and out-and-out selling. The difference is that these magazines are aimed at twelve-year-olds, readers who don't understand that the "Technicolor dress" is unattainable.

These same magazines frequently include accounts of adolescents in other countries in an attempt to show their similarity to American teens: their cache-mongering and the tribal subdivisions between punk and preppy and hip hop kids in Cape Town or Sao Paolo. And while these cool hunting articles in American teen magazines convince American teens that all the world is a mall promoting a global youth materialism and homogeneity, these international fashion round-ups also reflect a world-wide teen consumerism and an erasure of national youth identity. In recession-era Japan, fashion photographers lurk in the trendy Harajuku neighborhood, ready to capture images of modish teens who, in turn, may well have received their cues from half a dozen teen girl fashion magazines with such names as *Style on the Street* and *Cutie*. (Scholars have theorized that global luxury brands such as Louis Vuitton and Hermes are particularly desirable to contemporary Japan's young "trend slaves" because they help build a generation's fragile self-confidence about the future). In England, tweenies and teens become the targets of pitches offering to add extras on their already ubiquitous brand-name mobile phones, plusses such as celebrity voice mail and ring tones; and the kids buy in. In Australia, a newspaper columnist dubbed selling to kids in his country nothing less than "corporate pedophilia." In Canada, a recent study by Laval University in Quebec found that their sample group of rich and poor kids had an equal and unslakeable thirst for designer clothes.

In 2002, the government in South Korea decided to create regulations for issuing credit cards to minors. The rulings were necessitated by a wave of robberies by unemployed teenagers seeking to steal money to pay off credit card debt. The credit card companies created the situation in the first place by competing to *issue* cards to unemployed teenagers and college students, jobless kids who later turned to crime in desperation. A resulting bill prevents the issuance of credit cards to those under the age of twenty without their parents' consent.

WELCOME TO THE DOLLHOUSE

The American and international teenage buying public has been a long time in the making. Marketers discovered, or invented, the American teen market during World War II and the early postwar era. They argued that teens would be spending their parents' money on movies, cosmetics, and records. In 1945, *Seventeen* wrote memos to advertisers promising that teen girls were "copycats" who could be trusted to imitate one another by wearing the same clothes and eating the same food. *Seventeen* also set in motion a classic advertising paradigm. The magazine assured its advertisers that a few ads in *Seventeen* would pay rich rewards later by sowing the seeds of desire within the girls for certain linens or kinds of china when they got married. Marketers still believe in the basic truth of the axiom "get 'em while they're young."

Marketing to kids took off in the 1980s, in the wake of two important events. The first was the release and overwhelming successes of the films *Jaws* in 1975 and *Star Wars* in 1977. Youth-oriented blockbusters, it turned out, could sell not just enormous numbers of tickets but also a huge and varied assortment of ancillary branded products, everything from action figures to bed sheets. The second important event occurred in 1978, when the Federal Trade Commission attempted to impose regulations regarding restrictions on child-oriented ads. Congress blocked it, claiming that its emphasis on unfair advertising was too vague. In the decades following, an utter lack of regulation ineluctably led to the widespread flogging of kiddy blockbuster toys and games and the huge success of products related to the Teenage Mutant Ninja Turtles.

With the stakes rising, marketers began plumbing kids' minds, recognizing for the first time the full extent of the potential monetary gains children had to offer. These kids were called "skippies" (school kids with purchasing power). Veteran marketer Peter Zollo has written that the idea of kids as worthy targets was so new back then that he had to persuade advertisers that skippies were a viable enough bracket even to bother researching.

Branding slowed during the economic recession of the late 1980s and early 1990s. But when the economy began to stir to life, branding returned, and with a vengeance. Corporations eager to gain a foothold went on the attack through the aggressive marketing of designer labels. The economy was growing fast, but ad spending grew faster. In 1991, ad spending in the United States equaled $126.4 billion; in 1994, it equaled $150 billion.

Given all the goods jostling for consumer attention, branding became one of the necessities for making products stick in consumers' minds. The companies doing the best were those that had over the years built up a strong brand and recognizable identity. Competition also led marketers to deploy ever more sophisticated and innovative sales techniques.

CRUEL STORY OF YOUTH

The language of teen marketing is now so refined that it resembles youth sociology and psychology. One difference is, of course, its intent. Academic writing on adolescence has, for at least a century, been interested in either teens' liberation or self-betterment by way of moral guidance from the family, the teacher, or the state. The marketers who borrow the terms and methods used by scholars just want to sell.

In her 2000 book, *The $100 Billion Allowance,* marketing guru Elissa Moses breaks "teen orientation" and teen spending down into "me-directed," "other-directed," "nonconformist," and "conformist." Each category is further broken down into types of teen spending. These include "thrills & chills," "resigned," "bootstrappers," "world savers," "upholders," and "quiet achievers." World savers, according to Moses, include teen Brazilians and Hungarians. But although these "café altruists" are socially concerned, a marketer should not lose hope in their spending power. World savers like "piggyback" promotions, Moses writes, in which a product is marketed for a worthwhile cause.

The fancy language Moses uses echoes that of sociologists and cultural critics who imagine themselves champions of youth. Moses's terminology, in particular the phrase "other-directed," harks to popular sociology from the postwar period, especially the 1950 book *The Lonely Crowd.* Categories such as "mainstream" and "conformer" and "channeler" echo the comparisons within cultural studies of youth scholarship of the 1970s and 1980s. One of the classics from that period is Dick Hebdige's *Subculture: The Meaning of Style,* published in 1979. Hebdige claimed that the nonconformist fashions of 1970's Britain, such as punk, were not just irreverent posturing. Alternative style was part of a youth armamentarium, a defense against consumer capitalism. In contrast, Moses and her ilk deploy the category "nonconformist" style as another mode of teen consumerism, not a creative resistant force but a sliver of a market to be pandered to. Youth cultural studies of the 1970s, '80s, and '90s, which aimed to empower and elevate teen subcultures, now has an uncanny afterlife as mere spice at marketing meetings.

And the amount of research hours that go into these mercantile quasi-academic categorizations of kids is unparalleled. The advertising

firm Ogilvy & Mather researches youth by using the techniques of social anthropology performed by the Discover Group: They videotape
kids with small cameras in their homes, filming their product choices
and behaviors. Meanwhile, Teenage Research Unlimited (TRU) ped-
dles the ominously named *Omnibuzz,* a monthly survey of six hundred teens and a bonus segment of 250 tweens, all culled from 847
focus groups. (They are not the only ones to use this technique; so
does Ally & Gargano, a New York City ad firm, and various other
agencies). TRU company also provides a "Coolest Brand Meter"
(Sony, Nike, Abercrombie & Fitch, and Old Navy were tops recently). These youth marketers aim to sell their products. And they do
so even if it means playing on kids' fears of being social outcasts or
physically unappealing. TRU's interest in only the "cool" teens creates a burlesque of high school politics—one that shows up in teen-
oriented advertising.

GIRLITUDE

Pornography has also mainstreamed as never before in the decade of
Generation Y, and advertisers now pander to the heightened body-
consciousness they've helped create. The clothing company Abercrombie & Fitch's ad agency blithely told *Women's Wear Daily* that
teens "love sexy bodies and they're more conscious of that than ever."
A&F makes sure they are. In 2000 and 2001, the company produced
a quarterly magalog of underdressed college jocks, porn stars, and
couples and trios wearing omnipresent branded underwear. The catalog was so tawdry that it was encased in plastic and was, at least in theory, available only to those age eighteen and over. The outraged lieu-
tenant governor of Illinois, Corinne Wood, called for a boycott of the
company, which she renewed in the spring of 2002 when the teen re-

tailer started selling thongs featuring cherries and sayings such as "wink, wink" and "eye candy" to preteen girls. Although the Web site that carried the images of these thongs, as well as the A&F magalog, was attacked by moralists from the right on sexual grounds, to me the aggressive twinning of logos and sexual desire when marketing to kids seemed far worse. The clear message was that when you and your partner drop trou it had better be expensive trou—your underwear must have the legible letters of a good brand or you'll never get a sexy boy or girl to date you. I haven't seen a more blatant example of a rich corporation's exploiting teen horniness, as if an adolescent need only buy underwear to instantly attract partners.

BLACKBOARD JINGLE

Preteens and teens are not just cajoled by sexy ads and viral marketing in their private and recreational spaces. They are invaded at their schools as well. A growing number of high schools are sponsored by corporations. Teenagers not only play ball in gyms rimmed with logos but also spend their English classes coming up with advertising slogans for sponsors, all under the auspices of their so-called public high schools. One hundred and fifty school districts in twenty-nine states have Pepsi and Coke contracts. Textbooks regularly mention Oreo cookies, and math problems contain Nike logos. Companies from Disney to McDonald's promote themselves within secondary school walls by holding focus groups about their new flavors, toys, and ad campaigns. (Teens who register their resistance to the presence of sponsors at school can be punished for voicing their displeasure. In one instance, a student who wore a Pepsi shirt to a Coca-Cola sponsorship day at high school was suspended for the insurrection.) School sponsorship starts when children are very young, so that by the time kids are thirteen they are more than used to having companies and lobbyists pumping private interests into the curriculum. Recently, General Mills gave out free samples of Fruit Gushers and instructed kids to put them in their mouths as a supposed science experiment (the children were then asked to compare the sensation to volcano eruptions). Sixth-grade math textbooks, published by McGraw Hill, feature references to Nike and Gatorade. Exxon and Shell sponsor science videos. The American Nuclear Society hands out a brochure to schools titled "Let's Color and Do Activities with the Atoms Family"; and educational programs sponsored by the timber industry, according to one environmental science teacher, teach children how to visualize the thinning of the forest.

SELLING ADULTHOOD

Some of the latest extremes of marketing to the young involve pushing adult products upon adolescents, things that are jazzed up to appear young and fun. America's distillers spent $350 million in 2002 to sell "alcopops," sweetened, fruity alcohol that is ostensibly aimed at twenty-one-year-olds; but in the drinks' semblance to soda and juice and in their boppy names, such as BoDean's Twisted Tea, the products really target adolescents. Such drinks encourage an early adoption, to use the marketing term, of booze, and perhaps also alcoholism, in teenagers' lives. Similarly, the U.S. government, empowered to protect consumers, is not blind to the power of branding over the young, and it has enlivened its advertising to kids. Once the U.S. Army told teenagers to "Be All That You Can Be." Now it has become newly branded to attract youthful recruits. After September 11, 2001, army enlistment surged, but not because of 9/11, according to army personnel. Rather, it was thanks to the armed services' clever $150 million ad campaign launched since

January 2001, which carries the tag line "An Army of One." This ad is designed to pander to Generation Y's self-interest and taste, and, in the words of one potential recruit, has "real cool" imagery. But the attempt to win over Generation Y doesn't stop there. The U.S. Army has even developed a video game: a "highly realistic and innovative" first-person shooter game that puts a player inside an army unit. In a radio interview in 2002, an army spokesman described the game as one of the new methods the military was using to "reach young people" over thirteen and to "inspire people regarding their career choices."

OVER THE EDGE

Of course, all of this intrusive marketing would be fine—just the way the shilling game is played at this late date—if it didn't deeply affect teens themselves. The personae, self-images, ambitions, and values of young people in the United States have been seriously distorted by the commercial frenzy surrounding them. What do the advertising images of teens, breasts augmented and abs bared, do to teenagers? These images take their toll on a teen's sense of self and his or her community. "You have to be thin to be popular," one girl told me, and the array of flat, bare stomachs at her summer camp certainly backs this up. Other girls told me about their eating disorders and their friends' body-image problems. Their self-understanding doesn't change their behavior, though. They are like birds that know every bar of their gilded cage by heart. "Can you believe this ad? No one's body looks like that!" one fourteen-year-old told me, pointing to an ad in *Vogue*. "A bunch of old men are telling me how to look!" Thirteen-year-old girls expressed pained astonishment at "eleven-year-olds who get their eyebrows waxed"—but the thirteen-year-olds shave their legs every day. On Manhattan's Upper East Side, one salon runs a back-to-school waxing special.

Brand consciousness sets in early. One twelve-year-old murmured to me when a girl clad in Reebok gear passed by, "Adidas is cooler." A small child saw a friend's Paramount T-shirt and shouted "Blue's Clues!" She knew the snow-capped mountain symbol of the studio from the split second the logo appeared on the children's television show. A class of third graders on a school trip can almost all distinguish which beer brands had brown bottles (Amstel Light, Budweiser) and which had green (Heineken).

The heavy-duty marketing from the cradle onward has warped the social lives of today's teenagers and exacerbated caste snobbery in the classrooms. The standard "pretty and popular" refrain has changed. Now teens judge one another more for the brands they wear and how much money they or their families have. Girls ranging from Brooklyn Jamaican Americans to suburban princesses to Christian Midwesterners told me that if they wear "scrubby" nonbrand clothes to their urban private schools or suburban or inner-city public schools, they know they will be shunted into the out group.

"You know what you're supposed to be wearing. You see it on TV," says Lenita, who is from Brooklyn. "They advertise on the buses: Levi's, FuBu. You've got to wear that gear to be in the in-crowd." "Yeah, it's twisted. Clothes are very important at my school," adds Renee, a thirteen-year-old from affluent Westchester County, outside New York City. "Brands designate social position."

"What brand is that?" teen girls sitting in a New York City Starbucks ask as a platinum blonde woman in Manolo Blahnik heels clatters by. "Where did you get them?" The girls spend the next hour giving strangers in their twenties fiercely competitive once-overs.

The new brand obsession has also changed adolescent leisure time. Social-class pressures have intensified to the degree that middle-class teens now work to catch up with their wealthier peers. Laurie, a seventeen-year-old from Denver, worked four hours a day during her senior year of high school so that she might spend $250 a month on clothes. "People know who has money at school," says Shelly, clad entirely in Abercrombie & Fitch. "When there's a party, people look through each other's stuff and check out how much it cost. At my school, you can only justify not having money by being good at something else."

Today, 55 percent of American high school seniors labor more than three hours a day, while only 27 percent of foreign students report that they work at all. And all this hard work does more than just make it less likely that kids will do their homework. A study published in 2000 found that working is beneficial to teen girls only if the job is of a limited duration. Girls who work only a few hours tend to smoke and drink less and maintain more internal control. But girls who work long enough for it to interfere with their schoolwork tend to become depressed and self-derogating, and to drink and smoke more than their less-employed peers.

Work can be particularly hard on poorer kids because they are by no means exempt from the pressure to be properly branded. As Katherine S. Newman writes in *No Shame in My Game: The Working Poor in the Inner City,* the consequences of starting a life identified with low wage work can be serious. Poor teens have to "swallow hardship" at jobs at Burger Barn, the only jobs they can get. "Fast food jobs in particular are notoriously stigmatized and denigrated," writes Newman. "'McJob' has become a common epithet for work without much redeeming value." She goes on: A swathe of parents and politicians like to think that teen labor is an unmitigated good, instilling a work ethic and giving pubescents emotional ballast. In one Colorado community, tweens, but also their parents and even a local mayor wanted kids ranging in age from between nine to fourteen be allowed to work—although it's illegal. In fact, while teens are not supposed to work more than twelve hours a week during the school year if they are under sixteen years old, in 1998, almost 150,000 minors were found to be illegally employed each week.

The popular impression is that today's teens are capitalism's happy children, but as one educator puts it, American teens' heavy labor is the "logical extension of materialism." Some have described teens as a new proletariat, kids who work primarily to consume more goods.

Parents are also an influence on Generation Y's fashion precocity and predilection for high fashion brands. When I was a teen and preteen, my style sense was low rent; it extended as far as $20 canvas sneakers and $10 T-shirts on which a dark lithograph of The Cure was bleached so the band was *only* their hair. The branded generation's obsession with opulent brands, including Dolce & Gabbana, Chanel, and Prada is so strong that the kids I interviewed regularly spoke of the luxury brands Gucci and Chloé and Burberry as if they were talking about their family and friends. But the knowledge and fixation on high fashion is not just an interest in classiness and elegance evinced by lower-middle-class and middle-class kids. It derives from a related interest adolescents have in obtaining the trappings of adulthood while still underage. Millennial teens now wear junior-sized versions of the DKNY and Ralph Lauren garb that adults wear; in an inversion of the youth cult explosion of thirty years ago, when adults dressed in young styles, teens now aspire to dress as if they were women in their twenties. It is common for mothers and daughters in upper-middle-class areas to wear the same expensive brand-name clothes. While the mother strives to look twelve years younger, the daughter strives to look twelve years older. They meet in between.

2

From the Mall to the Fall:
The Teen Consultants

Amy is staring at a small snowy diorama in a store window: a random piece of white silk dotted with miniature artificial white trees.

"What are they advertising in that window?" she says, with full disdain. She's annoyed by elliptical, "clever" commercials. "I hate those ads where you can't tell. You know that Gucci ad with all the naked people clutching a bag? What's that about?"

Gucci would do well to listen to Amy's expressions of distaste. She's only fourteen but she's a corporate trendspotter. The company Delia*s calls her an "insider," one of thirty modish girls who advise the teen fashion brand on how to appeal to her and her friends.

Delia*s, whose 2001 sales exceeded $143.7 million, is using the kind of input that Amy and an ever-larger coterie of teenagers provide to keep growing. In addition to its girl insiders, Delia*s also conducts research among teen and tween girls all over the country, including the members of its "affiliate program," virtual insiders who post Delia*s logos on their own home pages as a sign of fidelity to the brand. From this research, the company has learned, for example, that teenagers prefer shopping in actual stores in malls rather than just buying online or by catalog.

Delia*s executives echo the sentiment of the higher-ups at another enterprise dependent on teen trendspotters, the magazine *Teen People:* Working as unpaid consultants is good for these kids. They are being prepped for careers in the magazine and fashion industries, say the companies. And they enjoy it.

Maybe so. But the insiders and trendspotters are also a symptom of the way brands now corrode childhood and channel incipient idealism and imagination into ad campaigns. Adolescence has always been defined by certain talismans—a leather jacket, or bellbottoms, or, in my early adolescence, Sassoon jeans and Esprit T-shirts—but the new teen-brand insiders epitomize the new heights that branding has reached. Once kids bought an article of branded clothing at a department store; now they buy an entire identity, a whole set of clothes by one manufacturer at that brand's ersatz boutique. Kids become Prada girls or Old Navy chicks or Pacific Sun, a.k.a. PacSun boys—and even volunteer their services to these beloved brands to show the extent of their identification and devotion.

Their devoted voluntary labor tends to bear the faint taint of exploitation. The big print of a *Teen People* trendspotters' ad asks for kids who have "something to say about what's hot & what's not" and who want free samples and new products and are willing to appear in a magazine. The smaller type reads: "Research results may be used for marketing purposes by *Teen People* and advertisers."

Teen insiders and trendspotters spend hours each week e-mailing their corporate contacts with suggestions about clothes and magazines. They test advertisers' new products—a lipstick that stays on for twenty-four hours, a fuzzy sweater, a TV pilot. They fill out advertisers' surveys, sit in on focus groups, go out for coffee with marketers and share their innermost feelings about angora.

This is not just idle activity. I met a Delia*s insider who had covered the latest Delia*s catalogue with ballpoint pen scrawls, quick notes such as "Arty" and "Jappy" next to certain pieces, and longer notes next to others—queries about whether the red midriff-revealing Bette corset has bones, what kind of weather the sleeveless cowl sweater is meant for, and how serious the potential is for sweat stains on the cream-colored Lonnie Tee.

The help can be vital to a company's campaign. When the marketers asked one insider, Josie, for example, for the size of her locker as part of product research, she cut off the line of inquiry, letting them know that "if they're trying to get through to older kids they should know older kids don't use lockers for anything but books." An adept critical thinker, her talents are now being used by a company to sell its wares more successfully to kids who may be less discerning than she is.

Trendspotters often become proselytizers for the brands they work for. When Amy's friends see her in Delia*s clothes, she says, she tells them where she got them and they suddenly want to buy Delia*s, even though these affluent kids typically consider themselves too ritzy for the brand. It's classic viral marketing.

Teens are eager to be trendspotters, and when they speak of their desire to be of service to their brand, they tend to show the same enthusiasm that accompanies the urge to be a volunteer for a "good" cause. But instead of putting that volunteerist energy to use at a charity or nonprofit, these kids search for an entity larger and ostensibly more important than themselves: their brands.

On one level, the desire to work for these companies is personal. The kids want relationships with cool adult professionals and they are flattered to be taken seriously by the marketing thirtysomethings. The marketers make the teens feel important (one teen trendspotter says she is good friends with the women at the corporation she advises; they attend her volleyball games and school plays). These adults welcome the teenagers' hand-sewn bags and trend ideas more than the kids' real parents ever would; and, to make the teen insiders comfortable, the marketers firm up the bond by sending constant e-mails and exhibiting much younger behavior than their real ages call for—all to better obtain and absorb their teen helpers' insights.

Teen product consultants are quite a large population. *Teen People* has deputized 10,000 of them and dedicates two full-time staff members to their care. One works as the consultants' editor; the other manages a database of teens and reaches out to them when events are coming up.

The reasons for this warmth are clear: When *Teen People*'s editor Anne Kallin Zehren calls her magazine's teen trendspotters her "secret weapon," she's using more than just rhetoric. The teens provide her with copy, advertising leads, models, and a specific kind of credibility. The magazine has built an entire trade advertising campaign around the trendspotters.

And the teens get more out of the relationship than just the attentive friendship of the adult employees. These kids work as insiders and trendspotters because their Generation Y's alliance with brands makes them part of the ultimate in-crowd. This has much to do with the glow that has come to surround brands in the last ten years. Top brands are like stars, and working for the brand puts a teenager in proximity to stardom, makes him or her a member of a starlet's entourage. A Delia*s employee recalls being on a bus with a bunch of teenage girls. They spotted the Delia*s logo on his bag. When he admitted he worked for the company, the teenagers started squealing. For the rest of the bus ride, the kids treated him like a celebrity proxy.

Scholar Richard Dyer describes the dynamic of celebrity, which resembles trendspotting, in his book *Stars:* celebrities themselves are so frequently described by superlatives in the press that the distinction between the stars and the superlatives dissolves. The stars go from being the most beautiful to the most generally excellent, "the greatest." Teenagers weaned on the star factory easily make the connection between star and brand. By this logic, the most famous brand is the greatest; and when teens fuse with top brands, *they* become the greatest, as well.

The new sense of importance comes out in consultants' self-descriptions. Amy talks of her work as a trendspotter as giving her the feeling of being "in the know" and "cooler."

"Advertisers take into account all the stuff you say," says another teen insider proudly. "I critiqued an ad's text and my changes got in there. We told the ad people they weren't realistic and the conversation in the ad was unrealistic."

"I keep the *Teen People* folks in the know, helping them understand teenagers' lives," says one trendspotter. "I informally tell them, 'My friends are wearing this.'"

What the kid workers get in return for their hard work are gifts that tend to support their sense of brand as celebrity. They may receive special invitations to events, often marketing tie-ins that promote the trendspotter's product. Trendspotters then feel included in a stellar arena, and the inclusion, like stardom itself, gives them what they imagine to be power.

Shop Girls

Megan is a seventeen-year-old trendspotter in New York who definitely thinks that brands are like celebrities. "I wanted to become involved behind the scenes," she says of *Teen People*. Since she joined up in 1999, Megan has participated in numerous brand focus groups, spoken at panels on diversity (where she, a white teenager, stressed that images of African Americans in teen-oriented ads should be "more subtle"), and addressed audiences of adult advertising executives at Revlon.

Megan indicates another reason for the work she does, as important an explanation as the brand-as-celebrity. Trendspotting, she says, gives her a larger voice in the culture.

"They showed me an ad that was so superficial, the girls emaciated, the copy weird," Megan says, with pride. "I ripped it apart, showed them how to make them more real."

Megan saw *Teen People* become a megabusiness, its reader base growing to 1.6 million in just four years. Since it emerged, *Teen People* has been followed by several other teen spin-offs of adult brand magazines, including *Elle Girl, Cosmo Girl!,* and *Teen Vogue.* The teen magazines have become more than ever the first stop on an assembly line of promotion and celebrity worship. And if they are to stay ahead of their burgeoning competition and remain popular and profitable, the established franchises such as Delia*s and *Teen People* must look to their teen consultants to keep their products and advertisements in teen-pleasing shape.

The teens themselves, while not fully understanding that they are being used, do tend to understand the contours of their "job."

"All the labels that work with *Teen People* are up-to-date—if they are not, it is our job to help with it," says Megan. She seems to have internalized the language of the company she works for, and with it the idea that she and her fellow trendspotters are learning job skills from their unpaid consultancies. Although trendspotters may learn certain editorial or pictorial or management skills, these skills unfortunately bleed into the teens' role of explaining to advertisers how today's kids can be better quarry or showing companies how to plunge deeper into teenage psyches.

Trendspotters also are sometimes the kids with the most critical eye about the social group. These are the Influencers, according to

Teenage Research Unlimited (TRU), the much-quoted youth marketing research outfit. The Influencers are that 10 or 12 percent that the majority of kids, or the Conformers, (again in TRU parlance) look to for their fashion advice.

Josie, eighteen, is an Influencer. It's easy to see why one of Delia*s marketing women "discovered" Josie when she was waiting in line to see the movie *K-Pax* in Manhattan.

"We looked fashionable, I guess, when we were at the movie," Josie says, shaking her long sleek brown mane and flashing a row of beautiful white teeth.

A psychiatrist's daughter, Josie enjoys talking to Delia*s about what they should do and being taken seriously. When I meet her near her school on the Upper East Side of Manhattan, she is wearing low-rider pants and pointy black boots and carrying a Dolce & Gabbana black leather bag with leather flowers on its lip. Through her garb and conversation, she displays her knowledge and awareness of fashion and her consciousness of the semiotics attached to social class. She tells me about private schools' annotated social ecology: "If you are popular and outgoing, you can get away with wearing clothes without name brands," she says. But if you are second-tier socially, "you probably need to be a *fashionista*." Fortunately, the compensatory flash of a Prada bag can do wonders. Josie's analysis is more or less correct; many of the teens and tweens I have come across who are drenched in name-brand merchandise are slightly awkward or overweight or not conventionally pretty. While many teenagers are branded, the ones most obsessed with brand names feel they have a lack that only superbranding will cover over and insure against social ruin.

Josie is very attuned to the nuances of branding and social life. She was born and reared in an upper-class community in which most kids attend private school. This is a brood hypersensitive to distinctions of style. Josie describes herself as "branded Uptown" by her school's "artsy" kids, although she counts them as her friends. Josie has had a glamorous adolescence. Most recently it included a birthday party at a commercial bar lounge for her 140 classmates—during which she slipped undetected into one of the chicest hotel bars in the city for a bottle of white wine and familiarity with a blonde teenager who appeared in *Vanity Fair* wearing a cowboy hat and little else. Still, unlike some of her classmates, who dress like little versions of their mothers and fathers in pricey Italian leather jackets and sweaters and may trade stocks and bonds, Josie likes rhinestones, *Sex and the City,* and giggling. She may be a satirist and a cultural critic when she describes her world to older women like myself and the marketers, but she indulges in all manner of teen activity. She is half teenage hotel bar habitué, half sweet-faced enthusiast. Yet for all the sophistication of her palaver, Josie, like the other trendspotters I spoke with, doesn't quite understand what she is participating in and the extent to which her "consulting" is a mind drain.

For Josie, the Delia*s women and I are audiences for her displays of social knowledge. But it's difficult not to think about where else Josie could be putting her razor-sharp intelligence, which at this point is mostly directed at the vicissitudes of labels and fashions. One of the most interesting things about her work as a brand insider is that while she puts in overtime for the label, she does so in the manner of a marketer: Because she is aware of Delia*s low standing among the in-the-know, including her classmates, she wants to help change the company's image.

"Generally people my age think Delia*s is gross," she says, although she wears a lot of the company's clothes: "I change them and cut them and make them my own." She also recognizes the dangers of a mass-produced aesthetic to the point where she's been tempted not to share all her ideas about style with the company.

"The whole point of being fashionable is being individual, so I did have a moment where I wanted to keep my T-shirt designs to myself," she says.

But that understanding about individuality did not diminish her desire to be a Delia*s girl or even a *Teen People* trendspotter (she is thinking of becoming one). "It's totally fine that they know," she quickly adds.

The world of teen marketing was smaller and gentler just a decade ago, when Josie was a child. That was 1993, the year Steve Kahn and his Yale roommate, Chris Edgar, started Delia*s. In 1996, *Sassy* magazine folded prematurely, and Kahn and Edgar bought the magazine's mailing list. They started hiring "girls" fresh out of (and sometimes still in) the Fashion Institute of Technology and New York University.

There were no teen catalogs and few teen centered stores at the time. The department store buying bureaucracy dominated. But Edgar and Kahn had watched the success of J. Crew, a catalogue line then aimed at teenagers' parents. They saw the possibilities and helped create the world that their consultants, like Josie, now live in.

"Teens and tweens wanted mail, they wanted attention," says Kahn, the company's CEO. "They were at the age when they were writing their first love letters. It was the first time they placed an order—kids would wait on the steps of their homes for their orders to arrive, and they liked that they placed orders with someone who was almost their own age."

(Kahn's insights were correct: one Delia*s fan of fourteen, who lives in York, Pennsylvania, described the appeal of the company's junk mail to me in simple terms: "I never get mail otherwise.")

The Delia*s catalog has grown to an annual circulation of 45 million. The company's huge database of names and addresses offers tremendous direct-mail opportunities. It is also very useful when Delia*s launches stores in local malls. But there has been a rash of other catalog-based and mall-based teen brands, including Alloy, Wet Seal, and Hot Topic. Therefore, Delia*s' need for consultants like Josie only increases; and with the help of focus groups and the like, catalogue companies can figure out how better to mine their distinctly emotional appeal.

For all her cosmopolitanism, Josie buys into the same brand insiderdom that the Pennsylvania girl who was so happy to receive mail buys into. But Josie, unlike that girl, is in the ultimate popular set as a Delia*s consigliere and emissary. She wants to be heard, but no one is listening but marketers. She is practically a scholar of fashion and social rites, but she still hasn't decided to turn the desire for an audience into a more developed aim than just being affiliated with a label. In a period when even upper-class girls like Josie feel like they are heard only by advertisers and teen television programmers, it seems that the expansion of focus groups and consultant positions for the youngest and most credulous Americans can only continue to grow exponentially.

LIFE AS A TEEN CONSULTANT

The swankiest mall in Manhasset, New York, is the Americana Manhasset, locally called the "Miracle Mile" because it is part of an area along Northern Boulevard dubbed the "Miracle Mile." The mall is where fourteen-year-old corporate insider Amy does much of her work. In the parking lot, teenagers swaddled in leathers and clingy shiny jeans jump from their BMWs and Saabs and race past us on their way to Barneys, Coach, and Gucci. The fourteen-year-old girls have plastic Prada labels hanging out of their bags; the foundation and powder on their faces is masque-thick. It all makes me rather anxious. Amy notes them and explains to me how you can tell which high school they attend by how "slutty" their makeup is.

The mall is a glistening parade of stores, the nexus of social meaning for Great Neck's status-aware dwellers. Forty or so stores, the color of bone, are guarded by a procession of bubble-headed street lamps. In the parking lot, I count twenty-two cars in a row of foreign extraction: Jaguar, BMW, a Mercedes SUV. The stores are essentially identical: ivory-colored rectangles on the outside, music-free high-ceilinged boutiques on the inside. They are at the highest end of the designer economy. There's a Barney's, where thirteen-year-old-girls alone or with their mothers are trying on Puma sneakers and $100 T-shirts. There's a Louis Vuitton store, a Prada store, an Armani store. There are no real places to sit at the mall and only one place to eat and drink here, which makes it unlike most middle-American malls; indeed, it's far smaller than the jumbo two-million-square-foot malls common in the United States. In contrast to those malls, the Miracle Mile mimics New York City's Madison Avenue or a *bon chic bon genre* Parisian shopping district, but it has no semblance of social life or urban history.

One thing the Miracle Mile has in common with most malls is its use of "adjacent attraction"; this is a marketing technique whereby the soothing light of a glass atrium or the seductive image of a pretty girl lures a teenager into buying an entirely unrelated pair of designer jeans. As architectural critic Margaret Crawford writes, malls use adjacent attraction to conflate the "material and symbolic aspects of 'needing,'" where deep desires for beauty, for solidarity with others, or for friendship, for instance, are equated with purchasing clothing or perfume. Customers like Amy suddenly want things they have never wanted before, in part because of the nonsaleable objects and activities that are routinely juxtaposed with goods that are for sale. The environment creates a mood of ambiguity and anxiety that can be released only by buying.

At the Miracle Mile, conversations tend to have the same ring to them. In Tiffany & Co., three sets of mothers and daughters consider bracelets and rings, the preteen girls begging for silver baubles and charm bracelets. "I want that, I want that, it has to be Tiffany's," one girl cries. Customers carry Tiffany's pagers, fifty in all, which they receive from the store's Ambassador service desk because the foot traffic gets so busy; when its your turn, you are paged.

"Eighty-five dollars for a bracelet is not so bad, Mom," the girl says.

At the Mile's cosmetics emporium, Amy shows me the high-end lip gloss she likes, Stila, more particularly a $28 rouge-and-lipstick combo contained in a little plum-colored or mauve plastic case—if Fisher-Price produced makeup, this would be it. It's round and childlike and looks vaguely chewable. I had recently considered this product myself for New Year's Eve, but deemed it too expensive. Amy is undisturbed by the price but, her chocolate-colored eyes flashing, she tells me with intelligent precision why the makeup is excellent. Many in her generation have a taste for upscale cosmetics; *Seventeen* now is a cavalcade of finicky, pricey beauty goods: ads for a Clinique body smoother, a special thong panty liner (the ad bears a shiny pair of buttocks), a Chanel perfume called "Allure," represented by a French-looking "magazine editor." Prompted by data indicating that girls are more likely to throw bigger dollars after upscale—*Seventeen* estimates that teens spend $9.3 billion on cosmetics and skin products a year—adult brands such as the ones mentioned above, as well as Estee Lauder, Mac, Bobbi Brown, and Christian Dior, have made forays into the teen market.

As Amy explains why some makeup is better than others, it strikes me that although she is an unpaid counselor to corporate culture, she is also still just a pink-cheeked child in braces who wears a fluffy yellow sweater and Nikes instead of heels because she feels she is "too young" for chunks or spikes or platforms.

Amy's parents aren't as flustered as I am by their daughter's fixation on high-end cosmetics. Amy and her mom are not pretentious in the way the other mother-daughter pairs are that one sees in this town, the tweens in precociously high-end gear, the mothers clad in the same designer goods. But Amy's parents are also obsessed with branded gear and they are pleased with Amy's work as a consultant because they consider it educational and empowering. In fact, it was through her mom that Amy became a Delia*s insider, by way of a contact made on the commuter rail.

Amy's parents are also invested in keeping their daughter up-to-date. "I told Amy these beaded bracelets were going to be big last year and, lo and behold, all the teens started buying them," her mother tells me. She has a bird-like quality—her hair is dark and worn in bangs, her face is thin, and she is a quick and lively speaker.

Because Amy's parents are both in apparel, they cater to brand awareness partly because of their profession; indeed, the family's favorite phrase is "fashion forward." But the parents are not immune to shock over the rapid acceleration of teen spending in wealthy communities such as theirs.

"Now, the kids want to dress like they are on the show *Sex and the City*," Amy's mom says. "I told a girl that Amy knows that if she wants to wear Manolo Blahnik she has to have a really good job in business and the social life that goes along with it. They want to wear the clothes of women twice their age."

For all her supportiveness of her daughter, Amy's mom seems a little taken aback that girls and boys no longer rebel against corporate culture and even work as henchmen and spies for clothing manufacturers, happy to assume the mantle of a brand, wanting to dress like rich adults in their thirties. She speaks from the vague sense that when she was young, she and her generation were antimaterialistic. (In fact, as cultural critic Thomas Frank has written, the '70s youth cult rebellion was actually a stage in the development of the American middle class, the beginning of the co-optation of coolness. This period of apparent resistance was saturated by the buying and selling of products that were thought to carry or reflect youth rebellion.)

Amy's mom tells me how she was the official Best Dressed girl of her high school class in the 1970s and how her mother was shocked by it because she wore jeans most of the time. "When we were growing up on Long Island, we never wanted to dress like our parents," she says. "Now the mall is full of girls who are buying the same designer stuff as their mothers."

But there has been such an intensification of youth consumerism in the last decade that kids are aware of consumer products at younger and younger ages.

"In fifth grade, I wore ugly clothes, quote unquote," Amy says. "Then a friend got me a subscription to Delia*s and everything changed." That "more popular friend" taught Amy about "good brands." It was only a matter of time before Amy got caught up in what she dismissively calls the "junior fashion wave," where "sixth graders had bags as big as a table and the kindergartners started wearing Tiffany's bracelets." That was three years ago.

"In sixth grade, some of my friends had cell phones. I didn't get one till ninth grade," Amy says, tapping on her Nokia, which is covered in a rhinestone cover she received from the "Delia*s people."

In this intensely pressured world, any reasonably prudent girl like Amy may well need all the social leverage she can get. It's cheaper than being the sort of girl who never wears anything twice, which can become dreadfully expensive if an outfit costs $500. One can smell the competition at Amy's town center on any warm Friday night. The girls milling on the sidewalk resemble affluent adults and carry Kate Spade bags. Tiffany lockets hang from their necks. Their jeans are Mavi or even Versace. Their cell phones are Nokia.

Their high heels may indeed be Manolo Blahnik's spindly and tee-tering. Amy tells me stories of girls checking the labels on a Kate Spade bag to make sure it was not a knock-off and teasing the girl carrying it when it was deemed to be a fake.

One gets the sense that for girls like Amy consulting is a way of defending oneself from the abrasive and picayune judgments of peers. And consulting is less traumatizing than trying to transform a child-like body into a sexy one at the age of fourteen so that you can don the prerequisite tight pants and tiny T-shirts.

Consulting and working as a trendspotter doesn't provide the satisfaction these girls crave, though. There is never proof positive that one is ahead of the fashion curve. Because she wanted to maintain this state of coolness, Amy discarded her expensive Kate Spade bag in sixth grade, a year after she bought it.

"I know I am ahead of my peers fashionwise. They are like, 'Is that new? I like your shirt,'" she says, her face framed by a rainbow scarf and hat ensemble. "My parents used to tell me what would be hip and I wouldn't listen," she recounts. "Then they were right about those jeans with the patterns on the cuff and now if they tell me a lilac shirt, I buy it and I am ahead of the curve."

When Amy uses the term *hip*, it has no adversarial, alienated overtones—it's a synonym for "latest product." Kids who call themselves hip tend to trumpet rather than bury their corporate ties; in this way, they show that they know what color will be in next spring.

Clearly, teen consultants are not working in a vacuum. They have come of age in an era when their loyalty is courted from all corners. The adult variation of the new consumerism is marked by a disjunction between consumer desire and consumer income. For teens, trendspotters or not, the new consumerism is marked by a division between an adolescent desire to emulate adult consumption and the limitations of adolescence itself, financial and emotional.

Teen Trendspotters
in the Age of Tragedy

For the month after September 11, 2001, "teen trendspotting" and "insiderdom" and "youth buzz" seemed like cultural signposts from another planet. We thought we would never go back to being interested in seeing Sisqo on the cover of *Teen People,* or in who the star of *7th Heaven* is. We thought we would never again care how much Britney got to sell burgers for McDonald's, or whether she had lost her virginity to Justin Timberlake and whether that possibility improved the ratings of her HBO concert. We now lived in another era, a precinct of elevation and suffering, and all the pap of teens appeared obsolete.

An article in *Salon* claimed that the "bright side to the obscene events" of September 11 is that Britney Spears and the Backstreet Boys, *Total Request Live* and Limp Bizkit, *Survivor*, Sony PlayStation, and 'N Sync will never be enough. "Everything changed on Sept. 11," the writer asserted, bringing about the "sudden realization for many that their current opiates were nothing but placebos." Others predicted the end of the teen-propelled reality television, writing the genre into the past tense. "On Sept. 11, Americans got a dose of true reality," an article in the *Hartford Courant* read. "How can people watch a show called *Survivor* when so many people are simply trying to survive?"

Within a month, though, the mourning was transformed into patriotism. Mall-going was prescribed as the contemporary version of planting the victory garden. Go to the mall, teenagers were told, along with the rest of us. Delia*s sold many T-shirts emblazoned with the Manhattan skyline and American flags.

We were asked to shell out cash for brand name goods. The newspapers offered story after story about the blessedness of retail

Americana. The *Los Angeles Times,* in one of its many consumer-as-upright-citizen stories, quoted a Marina del Ray resident who told a reporter that "we need to put more money into the economy now." The telling detail? The woman was "balancing a shopping bag and garment bag, while trying to stuff cash into her wallet in front of an ATM."

The kids got the message. "It's patriotic to shop," Amy tells me. Two of the *Teen People* trendspotters echoed the sentiment. Buying and spending on luxury goods were reaffirmed as the keys to citizenship. It was a message that the adolescents I spoke with in the months after September 11 took to heart.

There are exceptions. Katie Sierra, a fifteen-year-old tenth grader at Sissonville High School in Charleston, West Virginia, was suspended for her antiwar sentiments in October 2001. Those sentiments were expressed in a sardonic handwritten message on her T shirt: "When I saw the dead and dying Afghani children on TV, I felt a newly recovered sense of national security. God Bless America." But for the most part, the events of 2001 appeared not even to dent the psyches of a generation raised in an age of prosperity.

Around Christmastime, I mentioned September 11 to Amy and asked her whether the kids she knows go to the mall as often as they once did.

Amy described herself and her classmates as shopping no less than last year: "In social studies class, I mentioned the article about Gucci's designer Tom Ford from the *New York Times* magazine [titled 'Luxury in Hard Times']," says Amy. Her classmates shot her down. "We still buy clothes!" they said.

Josie also described her worlds as unchanged by the national mood or the economic downturn. She strained to think how her family has been affected. "One of my friends' dad lost a lot of money in the market in the last few months and now she takes her mom's 1970s clothes and cuts them up instead of spending money at boutiques," she says.

Since 9/11, *Teen People*'s consultants have said in surveys that they want ads to be more subtle. They want stores that are fun and friendly and that provide big fluffy couches and soft drinks. Teen brands are hoping that clever marketing and teen consultants might prevent economic fallout. Delia*s president Andrea Weiss hopes that teens won't feel the pinch as much as their parents: "They are more optimistic and they have more disposable income."

Teen People's publisher Anne Kallin Zehren also argues that teenagers' spending will be far less curtailed than the spending of their parents in a time of economic uncertainty. "They are the most recession-proof segment of the population," says Zehren. "If you think about it, parents would rather spend less on themselves than on their teens."

For a generation raised in an America where rich and poor are ever more stratified, parents work longer hours and more jobs in their efforts to maintain their status. The parents of the middle-class millennials have surrounded themselves with brand names and creature comforts, and they tend to fill their work-driven absence in their children's lives with DVD players, TiVo, and magazine subscriptions. They have taught their children, now teenagers, to "need" luxury products rather than simply want them.

"They have grown up during a boom time. They don't know what it means to cut back," Michael Wood of TRU says about Generation Y. His group's surveys have found that 47 percent of all teen income comes directly from parents. Wood's conclusion is the same as Zehren's: "I think that many parents will go without things for themselves before kind of putting that burden onto their teens."

For this reason, teenagers who have been protected by a decade of their parents' affluence will continue to be the most advertiser-friendly generation in history. Even as Kmart declares bankruptcy, as the Gap falls into itself, and as Enrongate increases suspicion of corporations, teenagers remain as loyal and as trusting as ever to "the idea of the brand."

Teenagers have come to feel that consumer goods are their friends—and that the companies selling products to them are trusted allies. After all, they inquire after the kids' opinions with all the solicitude of an ideal parent. Tell us how best to sell you our products, they ask. If you do, we will always love you.

3

Peer To-Peer Marketing

Jordan and Sidney (daughters of a longtime Mary Kay sales representative) now sell Mary Kay's new teen line of cosmetics, Velocity, at cheerleading parties and bridal fairs. While Mary Kay is famous for its Tupperware-esque cosmetics parties, events that well express the firm's middle-aged, tarnished-Southern-belle brand identity, the Texas-based company, which symbolizes its industrial-strength femininity through the trademark pink Cadillacs its best saleswomen drive, is now getting younger, looking to the daughters of its reps to help it shake its mid-life crisis. Mary Kay is now so assured of its teenage sales system that it has no plans to sell its cosmetics in stores while it can charge prices higher than typical drugstore fare: $28 for 48 mls. (1.7 ounces) of perfume and $11 for a lipstick.

"Our core market was baby boomers and we wanted to introduce a new generation of women to Mary Kay brand—many of our customers and sales women have teen daughters, a natural extension of the brand to reach out to the market," explains Rhonda Shasteen, vice president of global marketing. "Kids will pull out [our] product after gym class, start a conversation: 'My mom's a beauty consultant, I can get you samples.'"

Even Avon, a classic prim cosmetics line, which started around 1880, has now zoned in on peer-to-peer as well. In 2003, Avon will launch new cosmetics, body products, and maybe jewelry, for teenage girls. The plan is that junior Avon ladies will hawk the stuff to their friends.

Welcome to teen peer-to-peer marketing. It has been around a long time and in many forms, from the girls rounded up and paid to scream for Frank Sinatra in the 1930s to the hard sell of hip-hop and assorted accessories by way of so-called street teams, or marketing youth gangs, that have advertised certain products since the 1980s. (Street teams are sometimes cast to make sure they are "on message"; for marketing the movie *The Fast and the Furious* at clubs and concerts, for instance, the marketers were carefully examined to make sure they looked just like the film's street racers.)

In 1956, Hires Root Beer may have been the first brand to use what was then called "youth-to-youth" promotion. Hires went from high school to high school, at each place choosing a leading female to pitch the product to her classmates. The Hires girls were instructed to contact the concession managers for school sports events, as well as the managers of drugstores and grocery stores near the school and tell them how great Hires Root Beer was and how much kids liked it. They were asked to sell Hires at school events. Most important, the girls were told to hold Hires Root Beer parties, where they were to introduce other students to Hires and keep a record of their classmates' feedback about the product.

That story seems quaint now. So, perhaps, does a more modern technique called "seeding," which involves giving away merchandise to a high school's most popular cliques in the hopes the brand will spread like wildfire among the in-crowd's teen fashion followers. The seeding of Converse sneakers at one high school, supposedly in California in the 1980s, is the stuff of legend—the subsequent Converse craze during that decade is one of the teen marketer's most cherished narrative, along with a similar distribution of Nike products.

There's nothing quaint about the enormous and relentless peer-to-peer programs directed at today's teens. The most obvious aspect is the use of teen and just post-teen celebrities: Britney Spears peddling Clairol shampoo, Polaroid cameras, McDonald's fast food, and Pepsi, which can presumably be bought in school-sponsored soda machines lining high school hallways. Venus Williams hawks Reebok (she had a $40 million contract at age twenty), her younger sister Serena sells Puma gear (a $12 million contract). The Williams girls are now playing out their three-year contract with Avon. Incidentally, they also do Wrigley's and Sega.

The Internet is also a force for peer-to-peer marketing, stretching the boundaries between kids sharing their fandom with one another and doing the work of companies for them. Given that teens now spend so many hours surfing the Web, and far fewer hours watching television than previous generations, it's not surprising that intense peer-to-peer promoting has emerged and flowered online, a result of the millennial ascendance of word-of-mouth popular sites such as Napster and AllAdvantage.

One groundbreaking Web peer-to-peer marketing maneuver was the brainchild of M80, an entertainment marketing firm. In 2000, teen Carrie was one of M80's minions. Brown haired, blue eyed, and pale skinned, she calls herself average. She lives in a town in Canada best known for its snowy season. But Carrie is exceptional in one way: She is a huge fan of the Backstreet Boy; such a big fan that she joined a Backstreet Boys street team online. Carrie now felt at one with her gods, those five Boys—Kevin Richardson, Howard "Howie D." Dorough, Alexander James McLean, Brian Littrell, and Nick Carter, whose songs promised her and all the other teens and tweens the possibility of endless love.

Carrie and the rest of the M80 girls voted, as Carrie says, "several thousands of times for [the Boys' single] everyday," on Canada's Hitlist, MTV's *Total Request Live* and Web sites worldwide, thus ensuring the Boys' rise on the charts. The M80 kids didn't care that the BSB were the brainchild of music impresario Lou Pearlman, who forged them in his Wonderbread workshop roughly half a decade ago, along with 'N Sync and O-Town. Now the BSB are the gentlest of sexual threats—harmonized amatory cliches plonked into violin-laden ballads, accessorized in their live shows by the snapping of fingers and the swiveling of silk-suit-clad hips. But Carrie has been learning things from M80, such as how to convert her devotional responses instantly into the pidgin of publicity: "If you haven't already, go snatch yourself a copy [of the Boys' CD]!" she says.

"I joined the street team because I wanted to make a difference. I wanted to let people know that BSB aren't 'just another boy band,'" another M80 girl, Erica, says. "I feel that they are a part of me, because I've done so much for them . . . I couldn't tell you what President Bush is up to, but I know who was number one on last week's Billboard chart! Our [street team] e-mails discussed ideas to advertise the street team and recruit new members, and also the usual BSB news (chart numbers, release dates, touring, television appearances, radio, etc.)."

When it comes to the Boys, of course, there's no such thing as a street. The Backstreet Boys' street is the Internet. BSB crews received marching orders by e-mail from M80 telling them to call *Total Request Live*, the MTV show that in its promise of catharsis to adolescents is the teen Xanadu. Thus, MTV received hundreds of calls from girls begging for BSB's single "The Shape of My Heart." M80 encouraged its street teams to badger local radio stations with requests for the song, to wear the band's buttons everywhere, to put BSB links on their Web pages, to converse about BSB in chat rooms, and to lure other fans to join in their virtual promotional wilding.

So Carrie went online for four hours each day to crusade for BSB. She even hand-painted the title of the new BSB CD, "Black and Blue," on signs and posted them around her hometown.

Bolt.com is another site that has used peer-to-peer marketing methods, a teen Web site where members chat about topics such as "ugly people are cool" and whether camouflage pants are in again. In 2000, they had Bolt Reps, a hundred kids who encouraged other teens in their communities to register as members at Bolt and volunteer to pass out Bolt-branded promotional freebies at diners, schools, skate parks, and malls. They reported back to Bolt about events in their towns and local "cool" locales and promoted Bolt when the company came to their towns to sponsor events and the like.

Bruce, a sixteen-year-old from Houston, "became addicted" to Bolt.com and signed up for the Rep program. At several alternative music concerts, such as Blink 182, he doled out Bolt stickers and rubber-band bracelets.

"I've learned how marketing works as a Rep," Bruce explains. His voice is booming, penetrating, like that of a motivational speaker. A high school junior whose hobby is making horror and sci-fi films, Bruce says he feels he has learned skills that he will use later to sell his films. "Bolt has cracked my personal shell," he remarks cheerily. "Now I am able to talk to anyone and to get the word out about a product." He hawked the site at music venues in Houston, at the mall in front of teen hive Old Navy, and in the school auditorium during auditions for plays.

COOL HUNTING

The adults who market to adolescents and sign them up so they will share their intelligence are often called *cool hunters*. The term *cool* flatters the hunters' subjects, of course, and in the view of the adults, so do their business practices, through which they get kids talking about their taste-worlds. Therefore, the adult marketers say, it isn't exploitative. "They know I am a marketer and the girls don't care. They are fans," says M80's Vanessa Daffron. "When you are a teen, you want to do what your friends do, so when your friends tell you what to buy, it goes over very well." So, hoping they will spread the word, she sends her girls daily messages about "retail" and "spreading awareness."

"The kids are happy to participate [in focus groups]. They are happy to get attention and that someone cares about their taste," says cool hunter Jane Lacher, vice president of strategic planning and research for G-Whiz!, the youth marketing division of Grey Advertising.

"The kids would sit on panels for free if we asked them to," echoes Amanda Freeman, former director of research and trends for the teen data gathering company Youth Intelligence (YI does pay kids between $10 and $250 for their information). "We have a thousand teens on file and then we, like, have to replenish them each year. We joke that we 'do them' after we get information from them. Now we are asking them about the recession and whether the economy is changing their thoughts on luxury goods and logos."

"We act like friends and chit chat with them," says Freeman's colleague, Claire Ramsey, a research associate and now the director of trends. "I mean, they can feel the difference if they think we are stealing ideas from them and when we are forming relationships with them. We want to make them like us as we want the relationships to last."

What you notice first about these professional trendsetters, mostly women, is that they operate as faux teens. They tend to retain all the best mannerisms of youth and use their adolescent stylings to coax information out of the underaged. Ramsey and

Freeman, for example, present themselves with highlighted and mussed hair, moonglow eyeshadow, stiff blue jeans, leather boots with gold studs, and felt bags. Lacher, who is a lanky redhead and utterly peppy, seems like an eighteen-year-old, although she is in her mid-thirties. All these women are easygoing, amiable and articulate, helpful and buoyant, really quite lovely. "It helps our work that teens define themselves by their possessions," Freeman says. "They will say, 'I am Sony, not Panasonic.' Their favorite question is, 'If Coke were a person, who would it be?' I thought that was a stupid question, but they loved it."

All these teen marketers operate on the peer-to-peer method. They have to use this method so they can blend in at the diners and coffeehouses where teens hang out, stand around at clubs and outside schools handing out surveys, and entice girls to let them come on "shopalongs," during which the adult marketers write down everything the teenagers purchase at high-end cosmetics boutiques. These women visit teens in their homes and, while a mom vacuums the living room, for instance, memorize their young targets' toothpaste brands, their underwear preferences, and the bands on their rock posters. The marketers put the adolescents at ease by cocking their heads drolly and layering their speech with "like" and "whatever" and "cool." The girls love these women, and why wouldn't they? On top of all the attention, the girls are rewarded with new products from client companies—Sony Discmans, say.

Yet it's obvious that the cool hunters' jobs oblige them to make agendas that do not have the kids' interests at heart. The point of shopalongs is to obtain information to sell to cosmetics companies. The point of those Discmans is to have the girls take them to school and show them around; in this way, Sony's already overwhelming popularity will grow virally. Look at the Web site of the youth marketing firm Big Fat Inc., which gets kids to promote new movies online. The site instructs its workers on how best to "Get your target talking about your brand without even knowing they're talking about it . . . now that's real buzz." Big Fat hires popular teenagers to wear brand clothes in their ordinary lives, calling it "real life product placement."

The grown women who work at Youth Intelligence and G-Whiz! and teen girl magazines such as *YM* present their work as merely chic ethnography. And they're not without insights: they acknowledge they have an easier time reaching teens because of the teens' increasingly bleak and atrophied familial relationships. With parents out of the house, the social force of school and that world's currency—the in group's favorite commodities—now has a greater importance to teens than ever before. The adult cool hunters express guilt over this; they say they'd rather be doing their anthropological work for a better end than selling gear to pubescents. Then they shrug.

It may seem ironic, but peer-to-peer is based in part on the belief that kids are sophisticated. They are so knowing and cynical about advertising, marketers feel sure, that the best way to appeal to them is through their friends. Teens will see through the cheap persuasions and exhausted ironies of television ads, but they simply can't resist buying things their popular peers tell them to buy.

Peer-to-peer marketers are subject to no particular regulations or limitations. It looked for a time as though that might change. In September 1999, when the marketing of violence to teenagers was a hot-button political issue in Congress, Hollywood executives were called to testify before the Senate Commerce Committee. The executives were decried for pitching bloodthirsty media and for using peer-to-peer, among other maneuvers; for example, teens talked up R-rated films, such as *Disturbing Behavior* for MGM/UA, to their peers. But the hand wringing didn't translate into new regulations for selling to the underaged.

It's clear enough why kids are willing to be pint-size pitchmen. Kids do peer-to-peer for the same reasons they volunteer as consultants and shoppers: They mistake brand names for identity, or they believe their marketing puts them in closer contact with the bands, cosmetics, film stars, or Web sites they are hawking. Many were born after the Disney stores opened in 1987 and after brand-as-architecture and brand-as-destination became key to urban and suburban public space. Teens and preteens have grown up in a world where Nike is not just a shoe, it's a town, as in Niketown. Stores such as Old Navy and IKEA, which act as comprehensive experiences, present the good life as bargain basement. The branded stores, the head-to-toe brand loyalty of shoppers, and the ubiquitous product placement in teen films—everything from iMacs to Target stores—have created an overvaluation of brands in teenagers' minds. Being an unpaid salesperson is not a chore, it's a high compliment. In a sense, it provides these kids with a sense of selfhood before many of them have even recognized that they have a self.

M80 gets mostly girls to give away their labor for BSB (although for a harder outfit, such as Limp Bizkit, boys would be recruited more heavily). The reasoning goes that girls are more likely than boys to convey their tastes to their friends verbally. Girls are also more likely to use pop stars and clothes to anneal their fragmented self-esteem. It's the latter I'm thinking of as Carrie explains why she will "always" market BSB for no pay when called to. To Carrie, the hard-sell logo culture is central to her emotional life, and this is troubling.

"I like the Boys," says Carrie, "as much as I like my friends and family."

4

The Golden Marbles: Inside a Marketing Conference

"The influence of kids has expanded," said the pristine blonde ad exec. "Kids are the most powerful sector of the market, and we should take advantage of them." To many listeners, the words *kids* and *take advantage* spoken in tandem provoke a chill. But this was the Fourth Annual Advertising and Promoting to Kids (APK) conference, a two-day event at which the Golden Marble Awards are given to the best kids' advertisers. Held on the precipitous date of September 10, 2001, the fourth APK was celebrating marketers' ability to take advantage of the kids' market and also deploying their industry's favored neologism, KGOY, or Kids Getting Older Younger.

Of course, it wasn't necessary to go to the APK, held at the gilded Grand Hyatt adjacent to New York's Grand Central Station, to know that kids are being taken advantage of by advertisers. We also know that their exploitation somehow correlates with the evident reality that today kids *are* getting older younger, and that they are also estimated to cajole their parents and relations into spending another $300 billion on them. This group formerly known as children is now studied from every angle for responses to advertisements; one of the agencies being celebrated at APK, for instance, discovered through its surveys that more than 75 percent of kids enjoy silly ads. In short, tweens are marketers' new transitional objects.

And so I expected the worst at the APK, and I wasn't disappointed.

On stage at the Grand Hyatt, a marketer who resembled an overgrown all-American kid explained that six-year-olds have shelter and security but not introspection or self-consciousness. Another said that kids were between "a rock and a hard place, the rock of childhood and the dangerous place of adulthood." These developmental truisms were recited not as causes of concern but as sources of opportunity: openings for advertisers to better manipulate their targets. The audiences at the Marbles clearly loved the paeans to premature psychological development and received them with the same obvious pleasure with which they took in the colorful slide shows. When they were told that children like animation in ads, suddenly a sea of animated images played across a screen, a dizzying array of product shots and television clips edited together maniacally—red, turquoise, yellow. Cereal bigger than life mixing with Americana. The audience drank their conference coffee and watched google-eyed, their kid spirit visible in the little touches: the scrunchy hair thingies, the bright stockings. If you didn't look too closely, they could pass for the best-behaved high school sophomores on earth. Except that so many clutched issues of a youth marketing magazine titled, shamelessly, *Selling to Kids.*

"Kids are in the process of becoming," said Sonya Schroeder from the stage. Schroeder is an advertising sage from The Geppetto Group, a marketing company that creates the ad campaigns for Lego, Pillsbury, and many others. It seemed to me, as I listened to Schroeder, that her company's name, Geppetto, was one of many that took the language of youth hostage, poaching its stories and expressions of wonder. The Geppetto Group was named, of course, after the puppet carver in Pinocchio, the man who made a real boy out of a wooden puppet. Pinocchio is a morality tale about the importance of telling the truth. Is it somehow also a story that illustrates the power of advertising? Apparently so. One of Schroeder's Geppetto colleagues wrote about the meanings of the company name in a most earnest manner: "Geppetto loved Pinocchio unconditionally for who he was, no matter what he did. And he really saw him and appreciated him as a real child, bringing him easily to life. We approach brands similar to the way Geppetto created Pinocchio, by understanding kids, spinning our magic, and bringing brands to life."

Explaining the process of selling name-brand cookies to children as all about "unconditional love" and suggesting that advertising to kids is the same as "giving life" verges on a 1950s *Mad Magazine* parody of Madison Avenue. But then again, naming a marketing firm after a puppet master has its inherently parodistic side.

The Geppetto folks might manage to ignore the insalubrious quality of their company's name, but they were remarkably in touch with the emotional manipulation within their selling techniques. Schroeder, for instance, dubbed cereal "the ultimate dependency food." She decreed that a moral sense is at work in Geppetto's ads, and that she had found this sense particularly effective in tying products to youngsters' charged feelings about "reward and punishment and good and bad."

The audience, scribbling with publicity pens on Grand Hyatt notepads, nodded.

SELLING TO KIDS

According to scholar Lynn Spigel, American children first became a target audience in the late 1950s. Spigel writes that the television industrialists tried to frighten parents into buying television for their kids by way of ads. "Your daughter won't ever tell you the humiliation she's felt in begging those precious hours of television from a neighbor," read one. As Lawrence R. Samuel writes in his history of advertising, *Brought to You By: Postwar Television Advertising and the American Dream,* Advertest Research of New Brunswick surveyed mothers in 1951 and found that 60 percent of the moms said their kids wanted the products they saw advertised on television. In 1962, a marketing book titled *Advertising and Marketing to Young People* by the famed youth marketer of the period, Eugene Gilbert, recognized the value of licensing and name recognition in the kids' market, especially through cuddly familiar characters such as the Campbell Soup Kids.

By the early 1960s the category of "youth" was already associated with hipness, vernacular, and futurity. "Mature businessmen must start learning the 'idiom' and 'ideology' of youth or be left behind," as one marketer put it. "The [youth] trend is reflected in greater use of color, new materials and decorative treatments."

By 1964, an estimated $50 million was spent on advertising directed at kids. In the early 1960s, Eugene Gilbert's company, the Gilbert Marketing Group, held "Youth Market Clinics" for corporate types.

But it would be twenty years before marketing to kids found its avatar. Dr. James U. McNeal. McNeal's 1986 book *Children As Consumers: Insights and Implications* rocketed the kid business into an entirely new orbit by quantifying how much children influence family purchases (up to $130 billion back then).

McNeal, now a gentlemanly older man in Texas who runs his own consulting firm McNeal and Kids, sees the mistake of the early marketing models was their construing of kid consumers as "adult rational thinkers." When he spoke of his research in the early 1960's, he therefore encountered "bored people like the head of

Chrysler and head of Kmart," the sort of people who would later, of course, not be bored at all by McNeal's courting of youth.

McNeal's efflorescence started in the 1980's, he says, a result of children having more spending power, with their so-called incomes increasing at a rate of 15 percent a year. Suddenly he was a corporate consultant.

In 1989, corporations spent about $600 million on marketing to kids. In 1999, they spent twenty times that amount. Numbers of ad dollars are only one indicator of the excitement about selling to children. The size of kid business publishing is another. Retail anthropologist Paco Underhill, in his book *Why We Buy: The Science of Shopping*, suggests, among other things, that merchants should ensure that kids become media consumers as early as possible. He also provides a how-to. Books and videos, he writes, should be placed on the low shelves of stores, allowing kids to better "grab Barney or Teletubbies unimpeded by Mom and Dad, who possibly take a dim view of hyper-commercialized critters."

To this day, James U. McNeal is royalty among kid sellers. In his latest book, he writes of savings banks that target kids with special services, and stores "that have remerchandized their offering to get children's hands on—not off—products." McNeal cheers them for recognizing "that kids are people too." For McNeal, being seen as a human being by another is the same as being seen as a demographic.

"The plain fact of the matter is that businesses have only two major sources of new customers," writes McNeal. "Either they are switched from competitors, or they are developed from childhood. . . . Growing customers from childhood is a less common source of new customers, but one based on good business logic. If children are made to feel warm and fuzzy about a store or brand or product, they will bond with it. When they reach market age for that store or brand or product, they will logically migrate toward it."

At the APK, all followed McNeal's dicta about young brand loyalty.

"What we are doing here is starting in-the-cradle marketing: A toddler goes from Nick Jr. to Nickelodeon to TEEnick to MTV to VH1 to Nick at Night," said Donna Sabino, group director of research and market development for the Nickelodeon Magazine Group.

Tweens elicited as many developmental homilies as kids did. Tweens are "about" melodrama, about mastering rules, about the search for identity and a theme called "hanging out." On the Golden Marbles' podium, kids were no longer innocents to be protected, as they are in America's imagination. Their personal growth was constantly alluded to, but always in the context of their considerable buying power. Here, they were called "works in progress" whose penchant for buying "lip gloss, talk on cell phones, and wear pleather" at younger and younger ages made them terrifically attractive. For this crowd, tweens were shape-shifting miniadults, their little pockets full of dollars.

"The themes for the nine-to-fourteens are dual income families, single-parent families, time-crunched parents, and the world of media," said Sabino of Nickelodeon. (She wore little black glasses; perhaps because she was a researcher, she was immune to the requirement at the Marbles that speakers look and sound "fun.") The developments she referred to were Nickelodeon's move towards the tween market in spring of 2001 through the invention of TEENick on Sunday nights, in particular an animated series called *As Told By Ginger.*

The marketers, ensconced in a hall adorned with thick patterned hotel carpeting and gilt chandeliers, the crumbs of the morning's free conference breakfast still clinging to their laps, perked up when the presentation shifted to tweens, the new fair-haired category in the kid marketing circuit.

TEENick is aimed at those under fourteen, but it has "teen" in it for a reason, Sabino said. "Tweens want to think of themselves as teens." Needless to say, the efforts of marketers to persuade third graders to dress and act like the half-dressed cast of a teen cheerleading movie are a big reason ten-year-olds want to be teens.

At the APK, speakers made use of elevated concepts and terms worthy of social science. They quoted Piaget's cognitive development precepts. This made sense to me because these were clever people, around my age, who spent their days branding vaguely sexy clothes, lardy milkshakes, and bloodthirsty video games to children. They knew they had amassed some degree of leverage, and now they needed legitimacy. At any rate, each marketing outfit's reps needed to sound as surefooted and hard-nosed as possible, and they thought they could accomplish that through self-serious psychosocial euphemisms.

In line with this, Sabino pelted her listeners with statistics: One hundred percent of tweens watch TV, 87 percent listen to the radio, 85 percent play video games. The median age for a first solo purchase is eight years old. The average ten-year-old has memorized from three hundred to four hundred brands. Ninety-two percent of kids request brand-specific products. There had been an 8 percent increase since 1998 in parents asking kids about brands before they buy them stuff like sneakers. It's Adidas or bust for the under-fourteens, accompanying an increase of 17 percent in brand awareness of sneakers among that age group between 1998 and 2001.

As the facts flowed out, the crowd's energy seemed to grow. For these folks, there was nothing distressing in any of this; after all, they had been trained to believe that children wanted to consume as much as they wanted to sell to them. They had come to believe that becoming a consumer is a stage on the way to adulthood and also to citizenship. They were not bogeymen, merely

part of a larger system that believed the inculcation of brand awareness was up there in importance with teaching kids language skills
and career ambition.

"Kids noticed their classmates wearing the 'wrong' sneakers,"
Sabino said. The crowd tittered. "With the onset of puberty they are
learning physical mastery, and there is an emergence of social func-
tionality. For the nine-to-fourteen set, it's about where they are going, not where they have been." Like others of her ilk, Sabino
wrapped her company's motives in sensitive, psychological language.
The discourse within this professional claque tended to mimic the
tender loving corporate "stories" of teen brands such as Delia*s.

Then she projected an advertising aphorism on the screen:
"Media selection is a right of passage." No one seemed to notice
the goof. Could the misspelling of "rite" be an unconscious asser-
tion by a children's marketer that actual rights—free will, individual
choice, legal protections—are truly analogous to both coming-of-
age rituals and the choice of which television program to watch?

"As there's been a five-point increase since 1998 in parents' asking their kids' opinions on stuff like cars," Sabino concluded excit-
edly. "The car folks in Detroit are now trying to attract kids with
advertising. Kids have control over their parents."

In the 1990s, according to McNeal, companies began to really
see how to handle youth. The car companies finally understood
kids' influence on the purchase of a new car, the minivan. Now all
car manufacturers, he says, see kids as a focal point and target them
with ads in kids magazines, with tween spokespeople, like the Ru-
grats, selling Mercury Villagers.

The kid ad crowd murmured with appreciative interest: Kid
power was a familiar concept to these marketers, although what
they mean is purchasing power. Real kid power, the power to reject
brands and define themselves outside of commercial culture tends,

understandably, to piss them off. This group is annoyed that tweens, for instance, lack brand loyalty toward such venues as stores, restaurants, and malls. I could see that it might be difficult to work so hard to create whims and then find that the damn kids have whims all their own.

That irritation with their demanding customers burbled over in a teen-branding presentation by Melisa Wolfson, president and founder of Brains, Beauty & Bob, yet another marketing outfit with a kid-friendly yet obscure name. She handed out her "pop quiz" to the assembled youth peddlers with an air of resentment: They cleared their coffee cups to the side and wrote guesses for the brand names of the most popular scooter and slider shoes, the pubescent star of the television show *7th Heaven,* and which rock star dates teen star Rose McGowan (that would be Marilyn Manson). Wolfson completed the event by mocking her colleagues, chastising them for their sloth and cluelessness.

Wolfson's bio in the Golden Marbles program was not as bitter, but it still had an anxious quality. "Melisa has spoken at numerous conferences targeting teens," it said. "Researching and understanding the 'Teen Market' is not only her business, it is her life!"

THE ANTIMARKETERS

Outside the Grand Hyatt that day, a group of forty or so activists milled about on 42nd Street: They were antimarketers. They were fighting the Marblers with a counterceremony dubbed the "Have You Lost Your Marbles?" awards. Their placards read "Leave Childhood Alone," "Happy Meals Are Not Part of the Food Pyramid," and "Kids Are Not a Demographic." Some of the protesters were holistic bright-eyed young mothers, the sort who might also be breast-feeding activists or "lactivists," their young children in tow. A folksinger sang songs while plucking a guitar, her head-full of blonde dreadlocks resembling a weeping willow following along to the music. The most vocal group there, however, consisted of a collection of anticonsumerist academics whose aversion to children's contact with violent media has led them to become much more political and publicly outspoken than is the norm for those in the professorate.

"The First Amendment argument for the marketing of commercial and violent material to kids serves the interest of industry, not the interests of children," said one of these academics, Diane Levin, a professor of education at Wheelock College in Boston. In the wake of school slaughters at Santee and Columbine, Levin and other scholars have been called to testify before the Federal Trade Commission (FTC) and the Senate Committee on Commerce, Science and Transportation on the role of marketing and the correlation between media violence and children's aggression. In 2001, Levin and others wrote opinion articles and published signed letters in national newspapers as part of their more active role in protesting the selling of entertainment violence.

The "Have You Lost Your Marbles?" awards were the conceit of the Stop Commercial Exploitation of Children coalition, and more precisely the idea of James Metrock, president of the anticorporate organization Obligation, based in Birmingham, Alabama. Metrock was on hand to present an award—though not an award its recipient was intended to cherish. The antimarketers' awards recognized those among them who had stood up to the most unseemly corporate architects, and to the companies their activist literature called "the worst offenders in marketing to children." Metrock's award went to the Channel One Network, which produces television programming replete with advertisements shown every day to high school students and 8 million teens and tweens in middle school.

Metrock describes himself as "very conservative." Before he made himself the sworn enemy of, as he says, "businesses that advertise to children during their tax-payer-funded compulsory school time," he directed his rage toward a more Tipper Gore-ish project, the "proper" labeling of pop music CDs to protect minors from "violent and sexual" content.

Metrock is not alone in being a conservative mobilizing against kid commercialism. Within the generally left-leaning coalition that put together "Have You Lost Your Marbles?" and other protests like it, there are some conservative groups that tend to see kid commercialism as one of the many evils corroding childhood. Indeed, the campaign to curb the marketing of alcohol, pornography, and fast foods to kids has given rise to a bizarre conjunction of left-leaning liberals, among them Ralph Nader and the organization Commercial Alert, and archconservatives such as Phyllis Schlafly and the American Family Association.

The first wave of the marketing-to-minors backlash started in the early 1970s with a similar cross-hatching of groups. In 1972, the FTC accused major cereal manufacturers of spurious advertising, among other false practices (the case would be dismissed ten years later); and the kid consumer movement crested in the late 1970s with efforts to legislate marketing restrictions by the then-chairman of the FTC, Michael Pertschuk. Corporations responded by excoriating the FTC as "the national nanny," and moved to foil its efforts. Ultimately, Congress blocked proposed bans on televised advertising directed to children too young to understand the selling purpose and on the advertising of sugared food products to older children.

The growth of this second-wave consumer movement tracks the growth of corporate power and the intrusiveness of advertising aimed at children, according to Gary Ruskin, the founder of Commercial Alert, an anticommercialist nonprofit in Portland, Oregon.

He rattles off a list of recent achievements. The movement helped mount the massive antismoking campaigns aimed at teens. It prevented alcohol ads from reappearing on television in 2002. It stanched a drive by AOL Time Warner to put ads on the high school television station CNN News. It pushed through Congress the Dodge-Shelby parental notification bill, which requires parents be told if there's to be market research in schools their kids attend. And it won a big victory against school sponsorship in Seattle in 2001.

But even with these recent victories, the battle against the kid marketing industry has a David-and-Goliath cast. And on the day of the "Have You Lost Your Marbles?" event, the antimarketers seemed small and fierce rather than powerful. They were very pleased, though, when they gave the Inspirational Leadership Award to the Swedish government "for its leadership in the European Union to ban television advertising to children." On hand was a real-life Swedish minister, an elegant woman in her late sixties, who showed up in a tailored suit and stockings and explained how the Swedes had outlawed advertising to kids under twelve. Exhibiting the kindly hauteur of Ingrid Bergman, she joined the rougher-looking crowd. The minister's presence at the demonstration underlined one of the "Have You Lost Your Marbles?" crowd's major points—that many European countries are much more enlightened than the United States in their attitudes and laws toward branding aimed at minors. Sweden bans ads for children's toys, food, and electronic games, for instance, for children under twelve. That's farther than any other country has gone, but Sweden is not alone in its wariness about selling to its most open-minded citizens. Early 2002 saw a serious, though unsuccessful, attempt by the Norwegians to form a Nordic coalition against television advertising directed at children.

Great Britain is also considering stricter guidelines, and some members of Parliament supported a motion in the House of Commons calling for restrictions on certain advertising to children under five. The pressure in the U.K. is so great that media associations, in a sort of preemptive strike against their critics, feel the need to self-regulate with kid media literacy programs. One, called Media Smart, teaches children how to interpret advertising. France has also issued guidelines for ads directed at its most vulnerable citizens and is working to better regulate interactive ads aimed at minors.

The antimarketers at the APK were wide ranging in their targets. They presented a mocking "award" to *Teletubbies*, a program I had previously considered innocuous and even sweet. According to the antimarblers, *Teletubbies* is involved in toy promotions with McDonald's and Burger King, "while claiming to be a leader in the fight against childhood obesity."

The antimarketers had planned their response to the Golden Marbles for months beforehand. One strategy was to send protest e-mails to one of the awards' key attendees, Scholastic Corporation, to urge the self-proclaimed Most Trusted Name in Learning not to attend the event. Coincidence or not, Scholastic sat out the 2001 APK as sponsors, an occasion that the antimarketers claimed a victory: Scholastic publishes not only the wildly popular *Harry Potter* books in America but also magazines that are handed out in public-school classrooms and have a total readership of 9.5 million kids. The company has something of a plummy self-image—David Goddy, the vice president and editor-in-chief of classroom magazines, told me that his magazines were "informational, bringing academics to life, motivating young people by engaging them intellectually." Still, if Scholastic Corporation was sitting out the awards, it was certainly taking better care of its image than it had in the past: For four years, *Scholastic* magazine had carried an annual twenty-eight-page supplement from Discover Card called "Extra Credit," which sung the praises and the merits of card ownership in general and, of course, the Discover card in particular.

The "Have You Lost Your Marbles?" crowd then presented an award to the psychologists at Applied Research & Consulting (ARC), a New York–based marketing think tank. ARC sends researchers directly into schools to interview kids. The executive ranks at ARC are thick with advanced degrees, and it particularly galled the antimarketers to see this kind of expertise and training put at the service of Nickelodeon, Disney, and Old Navy.

Then a particularly enterprising academic activist, Susan Linn, associate director of the Media Center for Children at Harvard University, produced a duck puppet and a weasel puppet and presented the award for "best nagging research" to Western International Media and Lieberman Research Worldwide. "Nagging research," which the company claims is the study of what inspires the underaged to ask for a car, cereal, or sneakers, is summed up in *The Fine Art of Whining: Why Nagging Is a Kid's Best Friend,* a report describing the kinds of parents who will succumb to nagging. As Linn wrote of this degraded scholarship in *The American Prospect* magazine, the nagging report lists purchases most likely to result from nagging; these include "four out of ten trips to 'placed' entertainment establishments like the Discovery Zone and Chuck E. Cheese's, one out of every three trips to a fast-food restaurant; and three out of every ten home video sales."

Joe Kelly, Executive Director of Dads and Daughters, a group dedicated to limiting the influence of marketers on the lives of children, gave an award for distortion of teen body image to Reebok and its ad agency, Bartle Bogle Hegarty, for the "Classics" ad campaign, a print image of a bikini-clad blonde with a bandaged nose that suggested the model had undergone a rhinoplasty.

"Sexualizing kids in ads is against the law," Kelly said angrily. Pedestrians, tourists on their way to Grand Central, and workers from the big office blocks near Third Avenue paused at Kelly's outburst. Then they kept moving. Many of the midday Midtown passersby were parents, and they evinced more curiosity than they might have about other issues, but they still had places to be, things to do.

APK, ONE YEAR ON

A year later, the 2002 5th Annual APK event is a rather different scenario than the year previous, though no less onerous. For starters, the post- 9/11, recession-inflected APK is much smaller. One participant noted the size of the event had shrunk markedly. I estimated it was a third the size of the previous year's occasion, and the participants appeared older and more somber looking, in suit jackets and pencil skirts. Perhaps the economic downturn had drained energy from the kid and teen marketing dominion (even though the teen business itself has remained a buoyant sector). The 2002 event was also more decorous in tone than the year previous. Held at the Yale Club's Grand Ballroom in Midtown Manhattan, a room with a ceiling with the topography of a decorated wedding cake and a grand set of mirrored windows along one wall, the 2002 APKers struck a more mature-sounding and reassuring pose. "Kids are still watching over twenty hours a week of television and that's not all kids programming," said one speaker, as if to ameliorate anxiety.

"Do not underestimate the power of television, do not underestimate the power of kids," said a panel leader, adding that in addition to television their lives are "so much richer" than they were 15 years ago, what with the proliferation of youth magazines and Radio Disney. The notion of "enrichment" of any kind was of course a welcome one with this crowd, but there was a question in my mind as to whether any of these variegated mediums added to kids' lives. At a session entitled "The End of Advertising as We Know It," a title that was assuredly more a homage to the band REM than to Francis Fukuyama, the presenter David Bryla, Managing Consultant at the Zyman Marketing Group, also took on the more respectable tone of the 2002 event, asserting that brand management was an offering of "guidance" and "navigation" to the kid customers: "When you build a relationship between a child and a brand you can price-up," said Bryla. By "pricing-up" of course, he meant "charge more." He smiled at the gathering, his youthful brashness and brush of cropped brown hair reading as a cross between Young Republican and Young & Rubicam.

"What's in it for me?" kids supposedly ask, when they encounter a product, said Bryla, but now their preferences "are more perishable" and their "window for cool is getting smaller." In spite of the events new Yalie burnish, the marketers still advocated such techniques as "game room Internet blitz" brand-name "prizes at summer camp" and even, in the ominous yet not entirely clear phraseology of one of the companies' literature, "buying cool Midwestern kids."

But still 9/11 hovered. "Events will disrupt your routines," said Bryla, as an image of the fiery towers crossed the screen. "External events will often cause consumers to change their point of view of your brand, and you must change to adapt."

5

The Great Tween
Marketing Machine

A line of kids stands ready to try the Money Pit, a transparent Plexiglas closet from R.C. Entertainment. Fake money blows around inside it, dollars sticking to the clear plastic ceiling. Today, in a demonstration of the Money Pit's appeal, two men with tan skin, broad smiles, and dark eyebrows ask kids to step into the closet. The candidates are an eleven-year-old boy with glasses, a girl with braids, and another larger lad wearing a baseball cap. The second the machine is turned on, and they all jump up in unison for the bucks, while trying to catch them with their hands and a baseball cap and squealing.

"You have to get the kids one of the booths for their *bar mitzvah,*" says Robert Greene, looking at the tweenies in the booth. One is his son, who has already started planning, two years in advance, for his bar mitzvah, the Jewish coming-of-age religious ritual on a child's thirteenth birthday that marks the passage from childhood to adulthood.

It's March 2002, and I'm at a party-planning showcase in three giant rooms of the Marriott Hotel in Uniondale, New York, on the edge of Long Island. Secular diversions such as the Money Pit, which comes with a $225 hourly flat rate, or the Show Me the Money closet, which has *real* money flying about for an additional $50 per hour, are now the norm at children's parties. Here and elsewhere, the Money Pit is a neat symbol of the new late childhood, tweendom, a sign that sums up the tween buyer's market, now so conditioned for rapacity.

Since the end of World War II, tween extravagance has become more and more commonplace (it is reputed that in the 1980s, one kid's bar mitzvah party was held on the *Queen Elizabeth 2*). But the last decade has seen a transformative amping up of materialism among tweens and their parents.

These kids are now a group so compelling to marketers that experts write about how to catch the tween market's dollars, as if companies themselves were the kids grasping for cash in the Money Pit booth. The most brazen example of this "how to" advice appears in the book *The Great Tween Buying Machine: Marketing to Today's Tweens*, by David Siegel et al. Siegel and his cowriters instruct branders to associate their products with "the tween centric of Popularity." It's a can't-lose strategy, they argue, for the simple reason that tweens are desperate to be liked. The authors note that that the tweens are the "heart" of the youth market: "too old to be a kid, too young to be a teen. Too old to want to be totally dependent on parents, too young to have a work permit, tweens can create a $100+ million brand."

Retailers have had a hand in the tween market's expansion—witness tween-only boutiques such as Limited Too. The Limited Too works in concert with tween media outlets: One line of clothing they sell is based on the new tween star of the Disney Channel show *Lizzie McGuire*. (Hilary Duff, the star of *Lizzie McGuire* sells the highly processed Lunchables packaged foods as well.) And the entertainment industry also sees tweens as a vast, still partially unexplored territory to be strip mined. The movie version of *Harry Potter and the Sorcerer's Stone,* for instance, was a gold mine of a tween product, and its success guarantees that studios will redouble their efforts to work the seam between kid films and teen movies. Never mind trying to attract tweens to soft stuff, films such as *Harriet the Spy,* one industry exec was quoted as saying; he is convinced that tweens like more "off-color" fare (they are attracted to supposedly teen or adult films such as *Legally Blonde,* which had a domestic gross of $94.5 million; in 2001, this film contributed to Metro Goldwyn Mayer's highest domestic box office ever, $450 million.)

It's no surprise that tween birthday parties and gatherings have started to reflect the gaudy and precocious new cinema. The birthday party showcase at the Uniondale Marriott is full of party offerings highly influenced by Hollywood. In fact, the oversized entertainments that tweens and teens and their parents have come to require in the last decade have helped to turn kid events such as bar mitzvahs, as well as children's parties and Sweet Sixteens, into theme parks. In New York City, wealthy tweens are given toy parties at F.A.O. Schwarz costing up to $17,500; at these soirees, buying is the theme. For the money, kids get The Ultimate Sleepover—fifteen hours for fifteen "lucky children," during which the kids riffle through F.A.O Schweetz, "one of the largest sweet shops they will ever see." They also play video games, make their own cosmetics, watch a movie in the "largest *Star Wars* boutique in the country," and go on a fantasy shopping spree. Teenagers wishing for a party (regression would be the theme?) can also rent the store in the evening for $15,000.

In New Orleans, the themes, formality, and color schemes of lavish Sweet Sixteen parties have started to mimic the debutante balls of the 1950s. In affluent suburbs of the Midwest, birthday party services start little girls off early with theme parties: One involves inviting the kids to don high heels and makeup and practice "ballroom dancing." On the lower end, at Club Libby Lu, a makeover chain for girls with shops in Illinois, Wisconsin, Missouri, and Minnesota, a typical party includes from ten to twenty-two girls at the cost of $20 apiece for an hour of getting their young faces powdered and their baby-fine hair professionally styled.

And, of course, bar mitzvahs in certain American cities and suburbs—Miami and Los Angeles, Westport, Connecticut, and Potomac, Maryland—can also equal the excesses of the New York–area celebrations. At the bar mitzvah showcase, parents are bracing themselves for exorbitance. They check out the now-prerequisite DJs and high-end stereo equipment. Meanwhile, their eleven-year-old daughters with lightened hair moon over the pale DJ who resembles a sub-par Vanilla Ice and shouts a quasi rap.

The vendors at this event are also boisterous, celebrating their wares to any parent or child who will listen. They are the small-time human faces of the more distant corporations that now compete for the tween niche's dollars—ultimately the dollars of adults—who now say they are willing to spend upwards of $40,000 on their children's birthdays and bar mitzvahs. As I walk along the thin lanes of stall-upon-stall at the Marriott, a woman in a glittering, beaded jumper proffers chocolate lollies shaped like Jewish stars, each with a digital and edible photo of a tween emblazoned on the front. Her neighbor argues that I should have his company make compact discs bearing text and a photo ("Totally Tara," read one). A now portly man guards a group of table settings. Each setting features some sort of counterweight, a string of various metallic-colored balloons hanging from it; one ensemble has a balloon in the shape of a handbag, a replica of a Discover card and a Master Card attached to it. Nearby table setting features a cardboard television showing pasted-on images from the NBC sitcom *Will & Grace,* a kid's face superimposed over one of the TV star's faces. There are child-sized wax hands advertised to be modeled on the tweens' own hands, each one holding a cell phone; and Fantasy Credit Cards, with photos of preteens printed on cards for Ralph Lauren, Bloomingdale's, and American Express Gold—mock passports from the country of the branded.

Shopping themes are a constant at these celebrations. At one bat mitzvah in Los Angeles, the materialist leitmotif was writ large: On each table a girl mannequin sat as the centerpiece, little Gap and Bloomingdale's bags hanging from her arms. Fittingly, there were bouquets of daisies where the girls' heads should be.

CLOSE TO THE
MADDING IN-CROWD

During the ten years following 1992, a parallel to the expanded bar and bat mitzvah industry emerged. The quinceañera business, an industry that caters to a Latino cultural milestone, a girl's fifteenth birthday, has grown exponentially. Once generally smaller affairs, they can now cost up to $30,000 (one "quince" party planner puts the average at $15,000 a pop).

Angela Rowe of *Quince* magazine, a trade journal dedicated to this burgeoning party business, remarks that quinceaneras have taken on epic proportions only in the last five years; she recalls how one father in Florida said that marriages come and go these days, but turning fifteen lasts forever. Planning for these soirees often starts when the girls are tweens, says Rowe, whose magazine holds focus groups with Latina girls before their birthdays to better target this preteen niche. (To exploit this market at younger and younger ages, marketers have devised Quinceanera Barbie, who comes in formal dress. Girls can now log on to BarbieLatina.com, where they interact with the Barbie and build fantasies about their luxury parties at least five years in advance.)

Families now often rent banquet halls, staging set-designed receptions replete with a dance choreographed specially for the birthday girl and her court of friends. Some girls get French manicures and professional makeup, and even a tiara (a crown alone can cost up to $300). There may also be a limousine, a video maker, and a photographer. In Miami, families celebrating quinceaneras may rent cruise lines for the weekend for relatives and friends. "Some of my more cynical students feel [quinceaneras are] a way for mainstream society to make Latinos spend money uselessly," Marie Theresa Hernandez, a professor at the University of Houston, told the *Houston Chronicle* in 2001. "There are instances where parents are willing to spend $15,000 on a quinceanera, but there's nothing in the college fund."

RIGHTEOUS PARTYING
OR RIGHTEOUS GIVING?

Some adults are less than pleased with the fake credit cards and shopping bags and the new, voluptuously mercantile character of what should be a religious event.

"My major issue is the commercial colonization of bar and bat mitzvahs; what should be a process has become a commodity to own," says Rabbi Jeffrey Salkin of the Community Synagogue in nearby Port Washington, author of *Putting God On the Guest List: How to Reclaim the Spiritual Meaning of Your Child's Bar or Bat Mitzvah.* "I hear children and parents talking about *having* a bar mitzvah when we should be talking about *becoming* a bar or bat mitzvah," he says.

Salkin sees the current consumerist relation to the ritual as partially an effect of a festivity business in which caterers are "cynically conspiring" to have parents underwrite events. The result is that events are both "more than they should be and less than they might be." Party planners foist themes upon tweens and parents that, in Salkin's words, reduce the coming-of-age occasion to "packaging." When his own son became a bar mitzvah a few years ago, Salkin recounts, his own family's attempt to have a "toned down" event was difficult given the high cost of even a bare-bones child's party today. "Affluenza invaded the realm of all traditional religions," declaims Salkin. "But conspicuous consumption with these events teaches the children that spending and having is more important than being—I tell parents to give to charities; *tzedakah* or righteous giving."

Eve Koopersmith, whose son became a bar mitzvah in the fall of 2002, also found having a low-key celebration for her child to be a struggle. "There are these out-of-control celebrations, where you deify the child rather than celebrating their becoming part of the community," says Koopersmith, a Port Washington resident. "At these parties, $50,000 is a drop in the bucket: It lasts five hours, which seems somewhat insane. I could get a new kitchen for that money."

Koopersmith, an attorney, considered having the sort of bar mitzvah advertised at the party showcase in Uniondale: one with a band, centerpieces, and a video montage. "It's a vortex; even people with very little money save for these kinds of ceremonies—everyone else does it," says Koopersmith. "You gotta have the video montage. We met with the video director and he said, 'Let me show you what I do.' He showed us a tape called 'My Bar Mitzvah!' that was the life story of a kid, put to music. Really, the child is thirteen and their life is not that interesting yet! I don't need that montage or that thousand-dollar-an-hour sushi chef!"

The Koopersmiths decided instead to have a family brunch after the ceremony and also take a family trip in their son's honor. Even that choice has been tricky, though. The children in her son's class, so primed by the party industry and perhaps also by their parents for the "blow-out," ask each other constantly about plans for their birthday celebrations and exchange tall tales involving games, DJs, themes, and the rest.

ADVANCED BEGINNERS

Tweendom's increasing market value is the result of a lattice of social change involving the kids' parents as well as the marketers' aggressive targeting. An increase in single parents, who often work long hours and are motivated by guilt to spend on their kids, has contributed to the rise in in-betweeners' spending.

That parental guilt explains why advertising to tweens is so popular. The easily manipulated tween buyer is now more able to manipulate an overworked parent into spending—out of the parents' shame over their increased absences.

At the party-planning showcase, the salespeople know all about tweens' ability to play on parental shame. Smelling money, the marketers are in overdrive; they call out their wares, the dried ice cream, the digitally photographed self-portrait magnets, not just to parents but directly to the tweens wandering around in their consumerist haze.

Lucky for the highly competitive bar mitzvah peddlers at the Uniondale event, the tweens' parents are also intensely competitive with other parents; after all, it was one of just three times that the party-planning showcase would come to Long Island that year and parents wanted to get the best stuff for their kid's fete. Adults invest so much in these parties, not only financially but emotionally, that one mother who finds most of the events to be "ostentatious" and competitive was afraid to be quoted in case it gave offense to "my friends or neighbors."

The tweens and their parents frantically push others out of the way to reach the stage where one MC is singing. They stage-whisper potential birthday themes to one another. Should they choose *Shopping* or *Billy Joel* as a motif? If they go with *Shopping,* there's a $200 poster that might be perfect, and, according to the vendor, it's very popular. The poster is a photo-shopped image of a *bat* girl surrounded by shopping bags from Abercrombie & Fitch, Tiffany & Co., the Gap, and Gucci. And they need to find someone to do the video montage of their son's life, a video that would make him feel as if he were on television, and a photographer to take their daughter and her friends to the mall and snap them by their favorite boutiques. The photos have to be good, because they will be shown to hundreds on the bat mitzvah day.

If they go with a Hollywood theme, they can get a poster that reads *Fight Club,* but with the name and face of the guest of honor in the place of the film's real star, Brad Pitt. Another poster promises to sandwich the birthday child's face between the legend "Thou Shall Have Good Taste in Music" and photos of Britney and 'N Sync. When I saw this, I felt there was something darkly mirthful about using religious language to celebrate teen pop at a nonsecular event, for the real objects of worship here are brands. So many of the posters here celebrate children's importance by connecting them to film stars and pop stars; the kids' visages are pasted onto the posters of the celebrities that the tweens have been taught to worship from younger and younger ages. In these posters, as in other areas of youth consumption, there's a slippage between "celebrity" and "tween" because the child aligns with "uniqueness" through tacit links to the spectacular star. "There's a cult of special-ness in the American middle class," says Rabbi Salkin. "Kids have to be special, the party has to be special, and then the families are unwittingly a partner in a communal narcissism, believing they or their children *own* the ceremony. It's *God*'s service."

TWEENAGERS AND SUBTEENS

In the early 1960s, the term *tween* didn't exist, although *American Girl*, the Girl Scout publication, addressed itself to something called the "tween-ager," which at that point meant girls between eleven and sixteen years old. In his 1962 book *Advertising and Marketing to Young People*, youth marketer Eugene Gilbert refers to the "subteen," whose ages range from ten to thirteen. He writes that a teenager, however, is "thirteen through fifteen, plus 50 percent of the twelve-year-olds."

"She is usually in high school, shops alone and is interested in sophisticated styles as closely related to the junior styles as possible," writes Gilbert. "Unfortunately for the teen, her figure still hasn't achieved the real junior look." Gilbert pioneered the sort of niche youth marketing we have today. He outlined what today's tween marketers, including Siegel, take as writ: "The subteen dislikes shopping in the girls' department for her clothes. She feels superior to the seven-to-fourteen girl." He noted that, as a result of the baby boom, in 1960 there were 37 million boys and girls ranging from five to fourteen. The retailer who taps this market, Gilbert writes, "can look forward to an unparalleled business potential."

Gilbert's clear outline for targeting the proto-adolescent market of the early 1960s wasn't taken up by his colleagues as a mandate. Ten years ago there was not a discrete tween market with its own stores—or as they say in marketing argot, "retail environments." Now even a chain like Target gives space to a junior department (which is often unofficially the tween department). There's also a clothing brand for tweens (Xhilaration), and special private-line cosmetics for girls whose skin is still child-perfect.

This new intensity in marketing to tweens has brought out the more venal tendencies in brand sages; they look at every place of children's vulnerability, searching for selling opportunities. Siegel and his colleagues write that ten years ago marketers committed a terrible oversight when no one considered tweens' health problems a potential market. He notes the increased incidence of asthma in kids—asthma caused by, among other things, a proliferation of toxic environments. Why not make the dull, drab extension piece to inhalers that help ameliorate asthma "telescoping and colorful," Siegel et al. instruct product managers to take financial advantage of a chronic childhood disease and improve the design of kids' medical gear—for higher profits. "Shame on the pharmaceutical companies," he concludes, insinuating that they should be more alert to the business opportunities implicit in children's frailties.

DAZED AND CONFUSED

Similarly, the bar mitzvah showcase certainly seems to me a whole new way to make Jewish Americans spend money. At the hotel, I met a gaggle of moms, all of whom grew up in the area. None can recall bar mitzvahs of this scope before the early 1990s. *Bat* mitzvahs, on the other hand, weren't commonly celebrated a couple of decades ago.

"This is a much changed occasion," says Ellen, the mother of two boys, one of whom is in the midst of planning his bar mitzvah.

"You have to have a DJ," says another mom, named Rhoda. "They run your party."

"You can spend $100,000 if you don't watch out," muses Jane. They note they have been planning for their kids' celebrations for ten months.

Although the mothers admit to minding the huge expenditure and the planning time involved, they don't seem bothered by an aspect of the bar mitzvah showcase that seems most striking to me: the prevalence of entertainment having "adult" themes. Dozens of gyrating scantily clad female dancers move across a stage in a frenzied manner worthy of *Flashdance*. A blackjack table, a NASCAR track, cars made of Heineken and Budweiser cans, mocktails, make-your-own music-videos, and fake tattoos—all these are on offer. The tattoos are to be applied by "artists" complete with plunging décolletage. I have lie reflexively and tell the vendors I have a stepdaughter: One tattoo vendor offers to place a temporary tat reading "Sexy" on my "stepdaughter's" shoulder.

These disconcertingly adult touches are clear signals of tween age compression and precocious sexual and material development that extends far beyond bar mitzvah planning at Uniondale. The Toy Manufacturers of America used to pitch dolls and stuffed animals to kids fourteen and under, but now the cut-off age is ten. (And now these toys may well be branded to encourage loyalty by the time kids reach the tween years: Tommy Hilfiger dolls dressed in logo-ridden "jet-set outerwear" and junior golf-club sets from TaylorMade.)

By eleven, tweens no longer consider themselves children, according to one survey, and they use such words as "sexy" and "trendy" to describe themselves. The teen catalog *Alloy* offers an assortment of clothing for tweens that "encompasses the look of the average fifteen-year-old," according to *Alloy*'s vice president. Why? Because nowadays, the common so-called wisdom of youth brands is that that tweens "aspire" to look like older teenagers.

The birthday showcase evinces all this premature product selling, a simulacrum of adult sexuality, synthetic poppiness, and "excitement." Those offering these precocious party extras may also be calculatedly tapping into tweens' ever-growing desire to be more mature. According to "Glide," an MC and owner of the bar mitzvah entertainment outfit Glide Productions, his dancers "reach the kids by being the party's big kids—we win them over and then they want to follow us around while we dance, like we were the coolest kids." Perhaps more frightening is Glide Productions' selling strategy:

Glide, née Victor Alicea, advertises for bar mitzvah services by going directly to the kids, winning them over at summer camp performances and fifth grade dances in public schools. "It's the best way to get them," he says.

The strategy of selling adult "hipness" is also evident at the showcase, where the DJs intone the words "fun" and "funky." They repeat those words so many times that I'm soon desperate enough to leave the place. As I exit, I meet a mom who looks as sick of the whole thing as I am. She says she's quite worn out by the hours parading past the booths. Her red-haired daughter eyes her mother anxiously, seeking approval or pleasure: None is evident on her mother's scowling face.

"It's very competitive," the mother says. "It starts in fourth grade and you have to plan for two years, book the venue and the DJ and the photographer and the theme a long time in advance. People give big gifts so then you have to spend more money on the event itself, like it was a wedding. I didn't even *have* a bat mitzvah." Her voice is flat, but her tanned face bears a wincing expression. She, like her daughter, is trapped in the new marketing creation, the great tween marketing machine.

6

Cinema of the In-Crowd

I was thirteen when I first understood what a teen film was. Knowledge arrived in the form of *The Breakfast Club*.

The characters include an indulged clotheshorse, a driven nerd, a vacant jock, a splenetic stoner, and an attention deprived Goth. It was 1985, and the film was the *Ulysses* of its director, that maestro of puberty John Hughes, taking place as it did during a day of detention in the school library. At first the film's kids are mere types. The jock eats six turkey sandwiches for lunch, the nerd toadies up to the supervising teacher. The stoner sneers at the princess for being a virgin, bringing her own sushi, and having a drunk, rich mother. The jock accuses the loser of lying about his abuse—that his father burns the stoner with lit cigarettes.

But suddenly the quintet comes together, dancing, implausibly, to new wave music that emanates from an invisible stereo. Limbered up, they tell all. The nerd (Anthony Michael Hall) announces that he brought a gun to school to off himself—he was failing shop and thus screwing up his GPA. The jock (Emilio Estevez) lets it be known that he taped a geek's "buns together," imagining that doing so would finally convince his macho father he was a real man.

The nerd, lean with a scraggly mop of blonde hair and buggy eyes, recognizes that his day of inclusion and quasi-Method acting will end as soon as detention does. Near tears, as if recalling his grade-grubbing harridan mom waiting for him at home, the nerd announces that they will all "become their parents": "It's unavoidable. . . . It just happens. When you grow up, your heart dies," answers the Goth (Ally Sheedy), glittery-eyed and black-clad, excited by her own bleakness.

At thirteen, I suspected my heart would die also, sooner rather than later. It's embarrassing to admit now, but the film spoke to me. Sure, it's overacted and broad, like a summer-stock theater production. But it also has the ring of a diary entry, of what life is really like when our parents or teachers leave the room. Raging against high school cliques and hierarchies, it puts forth an appealingly sappy proposition: that all strata of kids should unite against two common enemies, their parents and a future of soulless-ness.

BRINGING IT ON

Fifteen years later, few popular teen films would depict such moments of veracity, or have responsible, liberal reflexes to guide them. Teen blockbusters—among them *Clueless, Bring It On, She's All That, Legally Blonde,* and *Varsity Blues*—had become the stories of insiders: sports stars, beauties, rich kids, and cheerleaders. These kids live in the blondest, richest suburbs, suburbs without seasons. The characters have abs so hard and defined they seem to have replaced personalities. It's difficult to feel affection for these studs and sylphs and even harder to pity them; for them, MTV television is akin to the Talmud, and their bodies are so underdressed that they give new meaning to *pretty in pink*. After visiting this cinematic life-world, one misses John Hughes. In fact, Hughes seems the apotheosis of teen film integrity.

The new films' fascination with the high school in-crowd echoes the marketing recommendations of Teenage Research Unlimited, a youth marketing agency whose clients include Sony and Coca-Cola. TRU's goal is to snag the shoppers of the in-crowd, called channelers or influencers—"the cream of the crop," those "that know their status and revel in it," as the TRU spokesman has said. "If you can attract them, you have scored. The biggest kiss of death is for you to be a cool brand in the mind of the conformers." The taste of the popular kids will reverberate downward.

In *Varsity Blues*, the hero is an influencer, a star quarterback (James Van Der Beek, formerly of *Dawson's Creek*). At the center of *She's All That* is an influencer, the senior class president and soccer star played by the canine-ishly handsome Freddie Prinze Jr. The heroine of *Legally Blonde* is a Bel Airhead beauty queen named Elle Woods. Elle, played by Reese Witherspoon, is the best-loved, prettiest, blondest sorority girl at California University (this invented institution of higher learning happens to be an allusion to the college in the teen television show *Beverly Hills 90210*). When Elle goes to Harvard Law School, however, she is an outcast—because of the very qualities that made her so popular at CU. But she regains her influencer status at Harvard by applying her CU sensibility to a major law case. Her master stroke: keeping secret the shameful liposuction of her legal client, an aerobics instructor.

In *Bring It On*, the heroine is not just a cheerleader but a cheerleading *captain*, Torrance, played by Kirsten Dunst. Torrance struggles to keep her kingdom of cruel, anorexic simps happy—the resulting cheer-meets and cheer-offs are suffused with dialogue so excessively acid it resembles exchanges between drag queens in a mock cat fight. When one of the cheerleaders asks the team's hired choreographer why everyone has to go on a diet, he replies, "Because we're cheerleaders. We throw people in the air. And fat people don't go as high." When Torrance smiles winsomely at her crush while he watches her do her routine from the bleachers, her teammates are quick to judge. "You were having cheer-sex with him!" they say, aghast.

As a viewer shaped by an earlier teen film era, in which most films carried a whiff of after-school-special decency, I figured I knew what was coming in *Bring It On*. I expected Torrance to learn a lesson of some sort by the film's close, presumably some humanist nostrum about how girls of normal body mass are people, too. No such primer is doled out. Torrance doesn't muse about why she relies on pep and looks to get by but continues to let them work for her. (As for the film's box office, *Bring It On* appeals not just to lascivious boys but also to the prurient-older-man rental market; and no wonder, given the lithe teenagers performing deep splits and high kicks, their bodies encased in super-tight shirts, jog bras, colored panties, and even sudsy wet bikinis, the latter in the name of a car wash for, um, charity). *Bring It On*'s screen teens are more often than not what critic Pauline Kael termed "un-people." *Most* of the kids in teen films are. Where in a former era the pubescent stars might have evinced personal fragility, they are now brittle and paper-thin. Where they once were confronted with real-life difficulties, they now have contests, social machinations, and makeovers.

The in-crowd wasn't always given the benefit of the doubt. Once, the in-crowd were ice princesses and authoritarian despots: the girls in 1989's *Heathers* or the malevolent pranksters who think drenching a freak in pig's blood is funny, pace *Carrie*. In the former, the film's entirely unpleasant torturers, the all-named-Heather clones with upturned noses and flowing manes, answer the question "Why are you such a megabitch?" with the riposte "Because I can be." One of the Heathers demands that Veronica (played by a still *compos mentis* Winona Ryder) hold their hair while they vomit and that she join them in tormenting her former grade-geek friends. So when Veronica's gun toting hipster boyfriend J. D. (Christian Slater) poisons one of the Heathers, our heroine's joining an offing of the gorgeous tyrants is something of a no-brainer. J. D. puts kitchen pipe cleanser into a hangover cure, and then Veronica willingly forges that Heather's suicide note. The two repeat the murder routine with two more of the school's vicious snobs. One can't help but notice that the dying villains of *Heathers* are boys and girls who would now be the heroes of teen films. In fact, the popular kids' brand consciousness—Veronica curses them as "Swatch dogs and Diet Coke heads"—is part of their villainy. Viewers are asked to hate these iniquitous snots to the extent that they might think the popular teens *do* deserve death by industrial-strength drain cleaner rather than sympathy or worship.

And, of course, the outsiders that do exist in the films today are never as radically kooky as Ally Sheedy's character in *The Breakfast Club,* who shakes a head full of dandruff on her own drawing of a wintry landscape to make snow. If they start out disaffected and shunned, like the heroine of *She's All That,* for instance, we can be assured their marginality is only momentary—a quick costume change will seamlessly transform them into insiders in Act II.

The move toward the in-crowd emerges from an ever-increasing need to appeal to huge audiences. With films opening on twice as many screens as they did twenty years ago, expensive television ad campaigns and an aversion to risk have become the norm. Films are no longer allowed to accrue audiences slowly; for the most part, if they don't open with a bang, they die. And studios have decreed that teens in particular must be herded into the theaters on opening weekend or else. The twelve-to-twenty-four-year-old niche may constitute only 18 percent of the public, but it makes up 37 percent of the film-going public. This is also the demographic that buys tie-ins: Studios are increasingly engaging in a "synergetic" cross-marketing agenda by hawking soundtracks and other products. With so much of a sales burden now riding on teen cinema, it's not a surprise that films have shrugged off their loser characters; after all, outcasts are less likely to sell clothes or music than their popular peers.

DON'T YOU FORGET ABOUT ME:
A SHORT HISTORY LESSON

Of course, even the original teen pix were mostly market-savvy enterprises. The genre emerged from the film studios of the 1950s, when the industry discovered it had a young, eager audience willing to spend. Teen rock-and-roll films came to the fore, Elvis flicks and Frankie Avalon beach-and-bikini movies. For the first time, adults were offering adolescents a pop mirror of themselves on a mass scale.

Over the years, the teen pix genre morphed into the teen sex exploitation film, the likes of *Animal House, Porky's, Porky's Revenge,* and *Risky Business.* These films featured boys humiliating one another in the quest for "pussy" and trying to trip up fatuous authority figures on their way to the whorehouse. And the films did very well at the box office, setting the standard for the caricatured teen films that we have today. *Porky's* raked in $21 million in its first twelve days, and $105 million at the box office total, breaking box-office records in 1982. Its franchise prospered still more from the rise of the video rental (*Porky's 3* bombed in theaters, but it rose from the ashes as a home video). The *Porky's* movies centered on sex-mad Floridian high school students peeping at girls in shower stalls and bopping one another with a giant inflated condom. After

Porky's, filmmakers suddenly knew how to strike gold: They made popular films quickly and cheaply without the aid of stars or sets or well-established directors or scriptwriters; films whose plots could be described entirely by a movie poster.

Back in the 1950s, however, a more well-meaning model vied with the fun-in-the-sun teen pic for supremacy, the teen angst movie. The prime example was the 1955 classic *Rebel Without a Cause,* followed by other social-realist youth-gone-bad films such as *Blackboard Jungle.* They spoke to the extremity of adolescent de sires and violence, but also to adult fears of teenagers. In the lush *Rebel,* police officers act as psychologists to the burgeoning "juvie" population. In the 1950s, a period of relatively luxurious living, the youth-in-trouble was the counterpoint to the young consumer built for records, beaches, and stupid glee. As cultural theorist Dick Hebdige writes, "The two image clusters, the bleak portrayal of juvenile offenders and the exuberant cameos of teenage life reverberate, alternate and sometimes they get crossed."

Rebel informed films continued to appear through the 1980s, which in retrospect looks like a golden age for teen films. Teen films in the 1980s were often about kids living violently in the inner city, or simply living in comfortable towns on the wrong side of the tracks (a favorite theme of John Hughes). This strain included *Fast Times at Ridgemont High, Pretty in Pink, The Breakfast Club, Heathers,* and *Say Anything . . . ,* and ended with *Boyz N the Hood.* They did well at the box office: *Pretty in Pink* helped its studio, Paramount, get to the box office pinnacle in 1986. Despite the shiny clean appearances of these films' screen teens and the randy humor around their edges, the films were dedicated to themes other than which team would win at the football game or the cheer meet. Molly Ringwald in *Pretty in Pink* or Mary Stuart Masterson in *Some Kind of Wonderful* or John Cusack in *Say Anything . . .* were quasi outsiders. They were poorer than their peers, and sometimes seemingly parent-free, but also wittier and attractively subversive. At the end of the films, their triumphs were on their own terms, understood as testaments to the victory of personality and grit.

The teen film golden age also included stylish versions of teen novels by S. E. Hinton, most notably Francis Ford Coppola's *The Outsiders* and *Rumble Fish.* The central characters were juvenile delinquents, isolated lost boys (played by Matt Dillon, who handled this job in film after film in the 1980s) who found comfort only in other boys who had fallen off the grid. Coppola shot his teen films through colored filters and at oblique angles or in glowering black and white, underlining the teens' anomie (and perhaps also the director's frustration with making mere teen pix). At any rate, the teen films of the 1980s borrowed somewhat from the personal dystopias of early–1970s "New Hollywood," films such as *Taxi Driver, Nashville,* and *Five Easy Pieces*—what the essayist Robert Kolker famously dubbed "a cinema of loneliness." Now, teen pix steal their visual vocabulary from commercials and MTV.

In the teen-angst films of 1980s, the characters were capable of vulnerability, and vulnerability's flip side, defiance, which found its best expression in *The Breakfast Club.* A letter from the film's nerd that amounted to a Bill of Rights for white upper-middle-class adolescents reads:

> Dear Mr. Vernon,
> We accept the fact that we had to sacrifice a whole Saturday in detention for whatever it was we did wrong. . . . You see us as you want to see us: in the simplest terms and the most convenient definitions. You see us as a brain, an athlete, a basket case, a princess, and a criminal. Correct? That's the way we saw each other at 7 o'clock this morning. We were brainwashed.

Surprisingly, given the greed underwriting the 1980s, consumerism wasn't a big part of the teen movies of that age: Films such as *Porky's* were exploitative about sex, not money. "*Risky Business* aside, many of the eighties teen flicks expressed a yearning for a pluralistic school yard where wealth was no longer an impediment to the interaction of previously segregated social strata, where the jock could lie down with the geek and where the punkette could break bread with the princess," writes Jonathan Bernstein in *Pretty in Pink: The Golden Age of Teenage Movies*. Despite a penchant for too-obvious poignancies, the best 1980s teen films regularly depicted kids who rejected the established order.

The teen angst genre lives on today only in its most diminished form, in a take off of the very worst scene in *The Breakfast Club*. In that episode, the princess (Molly Ringwald) transforms kohl-rim-eyed Ally Sheedy. Using a normal amount of eyeliner, a headband, and a white blouse, the princess turns the freak from an androgynous ball of drama into a dull but pretty girl. That moment gave birth to one of the biggest teen film genres of our period, the make-over movie.

SCENES FROM A MALL

In 1995, director Amy Heckerling, who made *Fast Times at Ridgemont High*, came out with *Clueless*, which draws on *The Breakfast Club*'s makeover scene for its major subplot. *Clueless* was the first and best film of the new branded teen wave. (It was also a big box office success, which clued in studios that girls would spend to see themselves on screen.) The film set in place not only the genre's exaltation of high-end goods and opulence but also the genre's dependence on sharp-edged satire camouflaging an ardor for consumption.

Clueless's heroine Cher Horowitz is a Beverly Hills shopaholic: babelicious, surfacey, and affluent, played with good humor by the sunflower-like then-teen Alicia Silverstone, formerly jailbait in Aerosmith music videos of the early 1990s. Her upper lip is perpetually curved skyward as if there's something amusing on the horizon.

Cher is so fashion-mad that she uses a computer to tell her when her clothes match. Her nonvirtual fashion "project" is making over the new kid, a working-class stoner named Tai, played by Brittany Murphy. Cher is like one of the TRU channelers, introducing labels and cell phones to the conformers and the losers in her class. Most of her "work" with Tai occurs at the mall.

In the ten years since *Fast Times at Ridgemont High,* the meaning of the mall had changed dramatically for Heckerling and her teens. The Sherman Oaks Mall in *Fast Times* is strange to the movie's characters: a giddily forbidding fortress of mirrored walls, a place where one practices a future of wasting one's life in dead-end jobs or being hit on by older men. We understand that in the mall the nubile but naive waitress played by Jennifer Jason Leigh is inevitably quarry for predatory guys, and we aren't surprised when the circumstances lead ineluctably to first sex—and first abortion. In fact, the manic, estranged atmosphere of the film's mall breeds abuses of power in general, as when a teen wiseguy, lording his illegal access, scalps concert tickets to younger kids. In *Clueless,* by contrast, the mall is the film's safe space, homier than Cher's own home, a huge and remote white manse. Malls are "a way of homecoming to a self that has been lost," as one theorist wrote in the book *Lifestyle Shopping: The Subject of Consumption.*

The pivot between the depressing and heroic views of the mall can be found in a late 1980s film, *Bill & Ted's Excellent Adventure,* whose two eponymous Cali mess-ups retrieve Socrates and a host of other historical figures and bring these great personages back to the future in a phone booth; first, there's a stop at the mall before Bill and Ted drag their finds to high school, where the resurrected figures will act as their hosts' living history class presentation. Genghis Khan, Beethoven, and Joan of Arc set loose in the shopping center simply don't *get* that it's a place for shopping. Beethoven plays all the keyboards in the music shop. Genghis Khan swings bats and destroys a sporting-goods store. Joan of Arc leads a chaotic medieval-style aerobics class. Their antics underline the oddness of the mall and also that *Bill & Ted* is anything but one of the in-crowd teen movies. In fact, it's a high school loser's ultimate fantasy—passing history class (and passing life) thanks to the genial, dopey openness that would, in real life, probably pave a kid's self-destruction.

Bill and Ted's failure-as-success life plan wouldn't be permitted in today's teen cinema. In the six years between *Bill & Ted* and *Clueless,* all losers were sent to the margins. The winners were the ones sent to the mall. The mall would become, in fact, the ideal stage for the makeover film, which is all about normalizing social outcasts, turning them into influencers, and carrying them from the lowest high school social rung to the top. As Cher works to raise Tai's social profile, she acts as both stylist and publicist. She creates photo opportunities in which Tai will look "classic"—posing with a flower, paired off with a popular boy. And sure enough, Tai becomes a well-liked fashionista Frankenstein, so much so that she nearly supplants her doctor-creator.

She's All That is another makeover movie out to teach kids the importance of having fancy clothes and wearing good makeup. Zach (Freddie Prinze Jr.), a boy who looks good in sportswear, gets dumped by his girlfriend and then makes a bet with his jock friends: He can turn a loser into his prom queen in six weeks. Laney (Rachael Leigh Cook), the lucky loser, soon metamorphoses from an alienated artiste into a pert drone. The filmmakers, well aware of the new law of teen films that says all main characters must be style influencers, create Zach's sister (Anna Paquin), younger but more worldly, to make Laney over. A new look, an attitude adjustment, and Laney quickly goes from bespectacled neohippie to homecoming queen nominee in a short skirt. By the film's end, Laney even draws a parallel between herself and another branded film babe when she tells Zach that she feels "like Julia Roberts in *Pretty Woman.*" Clearly, the transformation recalls Liza Doolittle and *The Breakfast Club*'s infamous scene. (Critic Owen Gleiberman noted this connection in his 1999 review of the film in *Entertainment Weekly:* "*She's All That* is like a feature-length extension of Sheedy's transformation.")

The instant transformations promised by the makeover film seem very much a Generation Y phenomenon, an obvious way to speak to kids who have been taught to believe that respect and a new self are merely a new slip dress or new lip gloss away. But the makeover genre does have deeper roots. For one, it bastardizes the cinematic tradition of the "hidden" celebrity. As cinema scholar Stanley Cavell writes in *Contesting Tears: The Hollywood Melodrama of the Unknown Woman,* it was common in the films of the 1930s and 1940s for stars' faces to be "first shown hidden, or marred . . . perhaps simply as in the plainness of youth or of some other restricted office, and later revealed in the astonishment of its familiar power."

For Cavell, these films of physical reinvention are not just gaudy baubles describing the wish to be beautiful or to possess beautiful people; they are also morality plays that show an audience its beloved icons gone ugly and damaged. When the icon reverts, over the course of the film, to his or her naturally beautiful self, that transformation illustrates "the courage to become who you are," writes Cavell. Perhaps the most famous of these metamorphoses occurred in 1942's *Now, Voyager.* In that film Bette Davis plays the fat, beetle-browed Aunt Charlotte, but then she sloughs off her dominating mother. She transforms into the Bette Davis we know and love—a graceful beauty in the white, wide-brimmed hat, ready for an ocean voyage.

The transformations of *Clueless* and *She's All That* don't illustrate courage. Rather, they show girls willing to be tampered with by stylists. These girls believed that their stylists had a better grasp of what it means to look like a teenager than teenagers do themselves. The makeover movies claim that the girls being powdered and primped and branded are becoming their "true" selves. But the alchemized girls of the makeover film are in fact testifying to the power of constructed and artificial selves. Although the films give lip service to the notion that girls can find the courage to be themselves, they are in effect encouraging their audiences to be someone else, someone more suave, someone with straightened hair and designer clothes and overclass mannerisms. The real mission of the makeover films is to get across to their teen and tween viewers a limited notion of success. Anyone can turn into a popular girl or a prom queen, the films say. All it takes is a full commitment to beauty conventions and the high school brand economy.

CONSUMERS WITHOUT A CAUSE

On screen, fairy tale transformations don't happen by magic. They're possible thanks to such supporting players as Clairol, Clinique, Dr. Pepper, and Budweiser. Product placement in the movie surprises exactly no one at this point—look, Spider-Man is swinging past a Budweiser billboard in Manhattan—but the extent of it can still astonish. *Varsity Blues* is full of loving images of Coca-Cola and Guiltless Gourmet. *Legally Blonde* opens with a shot of blonde hair being combed by a hand wearing a Tiffany bracelet; the camera then moves down to caress a neck bearing a silver Tiffany necklace.

The blonde's college bedroom is full of other brands: issues of *Cosmopolitan*, bottles of nail polish clearly marked Clinique, a notebook from the teen shopping Web site Alloy.com, a Clairol Herbal Essences shampoo box (blonde, of course), a green case of face powder, also by Clinique. Outside her room, here's a sorority littered with brands: a Red Bull here, a Prada bag there.

But the placement of products is not just visual in the new teen fare. The films celebrate brands in their dialogue. Moments are branded: When Cher frolics in the sun in *Clueless*, she asks in voiceover, "Is this a Noxzema commercial or what?" In *She's All That*, Taylor, the film's self-proclaimed "prom queen legacy," walks through the streets carrying shopping bags clearly marked Clinique and Benetton and screeching that she could be wearing TJ Maxx, a low-rent brand, and still get elected. In 1999's *10 Things I Hate About You*, a girl explains the difference between "like" and "love": "I like my Skechers but I love Prada"; a guy recounts how he flattered that same girl by telling her he liked how her "Kenneth Cole shoes" suited her dress. And in *Legally Blonde*, the heroine helps to defend her client from a murder rap by exposing a witness—a pool boy—as gay after he makes a tell-tale comment that the heroine's shoes are last year's Prada. Brand knowledge is a major form of conversation, meaning, and whimsy in teen films; it is a symptom, and potentially a cause, of teen culture's growing obsession with acquisition.

The 2001 documentary *Dogtown and Z-Boys* is placement at a higher level. The film was financed by the sneaker company Vans as a ploy to get their skate shoes across to more teen buyers. The film is a story not only about the birth of skating but also about the birth of teen skater sponsorship: Vans has insured this legacy continues on with an exclusive *Dogtown* collection of sneakers and other gear. What makes the film so insidious is that it's a relatively legitimate and dynamic account of this historical subculture; only after you watch it do you realize it's all been a rather refined commercial. As Jay Wilson, vice president for marketing at Vans, told the *New York Times* regarding the subtle but constant presence of the sneakers on the feet of almost every person in the film, "We really try to connect emotionally with the kids and find new ways of doing things. We're getting more public relations on this thing than we ever imagined."

THAT WAS THEN, THIS IS NOW

Dim-witted teen heartthrob Ronnie "Bostie" Bostock is the love object of a scholar named Giles De'Ath; out of devotion to the young stud, De'Ath leaves the library and learns to love teen pix, fast food, and even life itself in the process.

It's the plot of a 1997 film *Love and Death on Long Island,* but it's also a story enacted regularly nowadays by American critics. Like De'Ath, film writers seem to have developed crushes on the Bosties of the world; at least that would explain why they are far more likely now to give teen movies positive reviews than they did in the past. The *Washington Post,* for example, called *American Pie* "deliriously raunchy," "[a] warped, hysterical and—believe it or not—sweet little gem of a movie." *USA Today* praised *Bring It On* for its absence of interiority, delighting that the film was not "heavy-handed about Torrance and her squad taking cheerleading so seriously"— the writer was happy that *Bring It On* didn't condemn its characters for believing that "winning a cheerleading trophy seems vastly more important to the squad members than getting the grades that will get them into college." Even the *New York Times* vouched that "underneath [*Bring It On*'s] tight acrylic sweater beats an unapologetically feminist heart."

Today, film writers revel in teen pix, but I don't think out of a real love for them. Perhaps it's because film criticism's function has shifted and critics have come to embrace "hype-culture." Once connoisseurs, they are now likelier to be more easy-going scribes who reward less-than-artful films as long as they show some iota of charm or spark.

For sure, the new critical laxity has something to do with the fact that our sensibilities have been forged on the crucible of the dumb and dumber film. And it's true that, compared to the lion's share of commercial films, teen films have surprisingly clever cultural allusions. For whatever reason, at least since 1989's *Heathers,* teen films have tended to include sophisticated and often rather meta jokes. In *Heathers,* the kids attend Westerburg High, named after the ashen lead singer of the band The Replacements, and the high school killer J. D.'s name derives from a wry contraction of "juvenile delinquent" (and perhaps also refers to James Dean and J. D. Salinger). In *Clueless,* the kids attend Bronson Alcott High School, named after a nineteenth-century New England transcendentalist who also happens to be the father of Louisa May Alcott, about as far from sun-and-cell-phone Beverly Hills as you can get. Clearly, there's something about teen movies that permits writers to flag their genre-awareness. Perhaps these brighter-than-thou references are also a subtle way of pandering to the film critics. To wit: *Bring It On*'s cheerleaders attend San Diego's posh Rancho Carne High School, which means "meat ranch." Self-parody on that level gives critics a different way to understand the film's predilection for low ogling angles of its underaged, undernourished cheerleaders, abs and panties exposed.

In truth, teen films are a genre that now offers critics one of the best opportunities to straddle the low culture–high culture divide; for instance, *Clueless* was gleefully based on Jane Austen's *Emma.*

That inspired, inevitably, a slew of teen films whose scriptwriters appear to be moonlighting at Cliffs Notes; 1999's *10 Things I Hate About You* was based on *The Taming of the Shrew*, *O* was *Othello* on the basketball court, and *Cruel Intentions* was *Les Liaisons Dangereuses* transported to a Manhattan private school. For critics writing in a period when the evaluative analysis of films gets short shrift, that the teen films contain allusions *at all* sets them above the pack.

In the earlier eras of teen pix, before critics inclined toward more generous readings of exploitative teen movies, there was a greater tendency for reviewers to call out the schlockiness underlying the weakest teen films. In 1986, the *Los Angeles Times* poked *Porky's*, writing that "even the box-office winners have been an embarrassment of riches that embarrass."

In 1973, the film critic Pauline Kael had the strength to find fault with the now "classic" *American Graffiti*, writing that she didn't care for the film's "pop narcissism." "It sticks to stereotypes—to adolescents who exist to be laughed at," she wrote, deciding that "mechanical people, including searching young men, are a blight on the movies, evidence that the filmmakers aren't thinking freshly, that they're resorting to the stockpile."

Some *teen* critics, however, still manage to question their film's shopworn images and perfumed, winner-takes-all cliches. Those teens who go against the flow and adopt a more critical perspective tend to reject the makeover films, offended by the beauty myths they peddle. For instance, the teen reviewers of *New Moon*, a youth magazine, write about *She's All That* as if it were rather nefarious, far worse than mere campy fluff: "This movie would be much less shallow if Zach were to be interested in Laney for who she really is, not because she turns out to be beautiful after a makeover," writes fifteen-year-old Christina Henry, who also felt there was something dangerous in having only "beautiful, big-chested" girls be popular, their looks the "only formula for having friends and a boyfriend." Lynn Grochowski, sixteen, notes that "when Laney makes the move to 'normal' it is only because of her new wardrobe, haircut, addition of makeup, and loss of glasses."

Emily Larson, eleven, writing in *New Moon* wondered about another teen makeover film aimed at tweens, *The Princess Diaries:* "Why couldn't the princess of Genovia have curly hair or flattering glasses? Mia didn't just get spruced up, she had to be physically made-over at the Queen's request! This scene was the highlight of the film. (Even the movie trailer contained this scene.) I wonder how many young girls, after seeing this movie, wanted to throw out their glasses, straighten their hair, pluck their eyebrows, or cover their freckles."

For adults, the films may drip with funny allusions and seem merely exaggerated to amuse, but for kids they are oddly real. One New York City teen I spoke with, now seventeen, was in sixth grade at a fancy private school when *Clueless* was first released. For her and the kids she knew, the film's ironies didn't register; she and her friends simply wanted to be Cher Horowitz. At twelve, she says, that meant talking on a cellular phone and buying things displaying bold-faced brand names. School was like *Clueless*, she says. "If you didn't have Kate Spade they made fun of you, especially if you were new."

There are exceptions, of course. There's 2001's *Ghost World*, in which two caustic, discerning, and unhappy teenage girls wander around a city: They're antibrand kids, a fitting and necessary complement to today's teen cinema. The girls rage at their town's faux 1950s diners and vacuous jobs at coffee chains.

Ghost World's girls articulate the promise of teendom: social mobility, restlessness, and overheated interiority. When I was a teen, I looked for films like *Ghost World*. I wanted to see movies like *My Own Private Idaho* and *Say Anything . . .*, which offered descriptions of *how to be* as much as *how to be entertained*. Lately, these films are in short supply.

Which is a real shame. Coming-of-age is just too good a theme to be squandered. For one thing, youth is nothing less than a metaphor for change. It's protean, not fixed. Think of all that happens in teens' mini-Edens, corners carved out in bedrooms and in parking lots and even in detention halls, places where teens are free of their parents' gaze. The new teen films fail to show those places. Why? Because there's an assumption that teens want to see the most bounded and superficial versions of their lives and themselves on screen.

But what these pretty vacant teen movies are getting wrong is that the coming-of-age stories in film and literature don't stay in our memories because teens are shallow and credulous, or because they have small pores and tan easily. It's because, as Patricia Meyer Spacks writes in her 1981 book on the literature of adolescents, *The Adolescent Idea: Myths of Youth and the Adult Imagination,* they "have all the emotional advantages." In teens, sentiment tends to outweigh thought, and adolescents' "exuberant psychic faculties" mean that films or books about teens can easily tap into the passions. Their cultural artifacts detail a refusal of ordinary life. Their useless love affairs, self-destructive paradises, and immoderate friendships seem melodramatic and strained in films about adults, but it wouldn't in films actually about adolescent life. But in the new teen films, the transactional, shopping-as-life story lines routinely get the better of teen exuberance and its cousin, emotional exorbitance. Instead of capturing teen life's present tense-ness, the films do just the opposite, creating characters who can't change or become. These characters are emptied vessels, slathered with beauty products. With such characters in the lead, it seems unlikely that mainstream teen films will evoke the cinema of loneliness ever again. All one can hope for, then, is a popular teen film that exceeds the cinema of the in-crowd.

7

More Than a (Video) Game

Skateboarder Tony Hawk maneuvers near a Quiksilver sign. When Hawk melons or lipslides on a thin ramp, the Quiksilver logo is visible again, on his T-shirt.

The action moves to Tokyo. When Hawk and his skater pals perform airwalks, they flash past the ubiquitous Quiksilver logo, which is nestled among all the other stickers and bright neon lights and the signs blaring brands such as Nokia and Jeep.

If you are watching this, chances are you're a tween or teen who has never done a kickflip, a revert, or any of the other high-flying tricks that Hawk and his gang are famous for. You might not even own a skateboard, in which case there's no particular reason for you to have strong feelings about Quiksilver, a manufacturer of surf and skate clothing. But in some very modern respects, the world of extreme skateboarding is your world—and perhaps Quiksilver is your brand—because you're playing Activision's 2001 game "Tony Hawk's Pro Skater 3" on your PlayStation.

Why has Quiksilver, along with thirty other companies, paid to have its logos planted within this game? Because video gaming did $9.4 billion worth of business in 2001. And because the Tony

Hawk games have had $450 million in sales since 1999. And because all those games are played more than once, which makes a big difference if you are a brand hoping to be embraced by young buyers. Will Kassoy, a vice president of global brand management at Activision, says that an advertiser who places a logo in a Tony Hawk game gets one billion "quality brand impressions" from teens playing the game. By "quality impressions" he means that teens playing the game over and over make deep positive associations between the brands and the game.

Quality impressions of a brand, Kassoy says, are different from other impressions because they arise out of the relationship between the video game character and the brand on-screen. "Tom Cruise drinking Coke in a film is a quality impression," Kassoy says. "Catching a glimpse of a Coke vending machine in the background during a Tom Cruise movie is not such a quality impression."

Tony Hawk's interacting with the Quiksilver store "allows for a deeper relationship" between player and brand, adds Kassoy. In "Tony Hawk's Pro Skater 3," these relationships extend to other facets of the game as well. Players choose what brand of sneaker and board the skater under their control will wear—maybe a Birdhouse T-shirt for example, Birdhouse being Tony Hawk's own brand. It is through processes such as these that companies and their logos go from what marketing sage James McNeal terms a blah "inert set" of youth brands to the cool "evoKed set" of brands (with a capital K for "kid").

"You see a board in the game that you like and you want the equipment: Birdhouse, All Starz," says Alberto, a fourteen-year-old skater, thin of frame and growing a light mustache on his upper lip. The game even sold skating itself to Alberto. Now he practices on the ramps near Yankee Stadium.

"All the stuff in the game, I want it bad but it's just too expensive mostly," he says. "Unless my mom gives me money." When his mom gives him money, he confesses, he "spends it on that skate stuff, the stuff that Tony Hawk uses." His friends Junior and Stephen nod in agreement. They are hanging in their local skate store, a downstairs grotto off the bustle of a New York City thoroughfare. On summer days, the store is full of boys in their huge pants, hair hanging down in coifed yet greasy strips, perusing the magazines and watches and sneakers. Certain brands of boards and shoes have a magnetic pull on the teenagers. Alberto examines a pile of boards—or decks, as they are known in skater lingo—covered with bright patterns and graffiti-ish letterings and eyes new wheels and bearings. The skate store's clusters of boys are for the most part wealthier than Alberto and therefore more invested than he is in *seeming* raffish and tough, as well as in feigning immunity to the video game ads.

"The Quiksilver sign in the game is like five hundred feet, it's ridiculous, retarded, unrealistic," scoffs Sean, thirteen, a freckly, still smallish kid who attends a pedigreed middle school on Manhattan's Upper East Side. "I play every day for like five minutes because of my ADD [Attention Deficit Disorder]," Sean explains. Despite Sean's contempt for the hard sell of Quiksilver, the brands in the game have made their imprint on him as well; indeed, he has no problem recalling the brands that appear in the game, brands such as Circa and Alien Workshop, the unaffordable skate gear that Alberto and his friends are programmed to desire.

"The games make you want to buy," says skater Mark Hermoso. Hermoso tells me he played "Tony Hawk's Pro Skater 2" obsessively when was a junior in a high school in Queens, New York. Now at twenty, he warmly recalls not only the game's fluid, easy play and "realism" but also the game's many in-game brands, some of which he had never heard of before he discovered the game: Action footwear, Baker skateboards. We are sitting in front of a glass case full of mirrory wraparound sunglasses; above us hangs a hanging skate deck that bears the legend Willy Santos and an illustrated ape with a somber expression. Hermoso, clad in a street skater's oversized shirt bearing a Senate logo and also the regulation too-big pants, tells me about his friend's thirteen-year-old brother and his friends, who "were even more affected by the game" than he was. They rushed to buy gear they saw in the "Pro Skater 3" soon after they started playing, he says. "Suddenly, these kids were like, 'I want that, I have to have that!'"

The captive audiences these games garner are not lost on marketers. Tweens are more likely to learn their fashion cues from a game than from television. Television watching has diminished among teens over the last decade. A recent survey of 12,000 adolescents found that teens spend 12.2 hours per week online and only 7.6 hours per week watching TV. And the attention of those kids who still watch television tends to be fragmented across many cable channels. What's more, kids are increasingly likely to be avoiding television advertising through technologies such as TiVo and DVR.

For smaller companies, this is great news. The cost of placement in video games is cheap compared to television advertising. Supplement the placement with some grassroots marketing and you acquire incredible reach. Quiksilver, for example, now puts kiosks for Pro Skater 3 in some of its stores. (I had the rather disorienting experience of playing the game at a kiosk in a Quiksilver store; in the game, the virtual "I" also shopped at a Quiksilver store for a brand-name outfit and board). In late 2001, in a nationwide example of guerrilla marketing (though certainly a sanitized version of it), Activision held a Tony Hawk Skate Free Day at thirty-six skate parks. The company announced the events through street marketing teams, Web promotions at skateboard Web sites, and direct mail postcards.

But video game product placement is not just cheaper and more *au courant* than television advertising. It's also more devious, because it relies on the ambience created around an item rather than a frank exaltation of a product's virtues. "Pro Skater 3," for example, gives Chrysler a new and much-needed jolt of teen rebellion when a large sign for the Jeep brand appears in the background while the expert virtual skater struts his stuff.

This kind of product placement goes back to the notion of brand equity. Lieberman Research Worldwide, a marketing consultancy, describes brand equity as a desire for products that are made to play into the "attitudes or beliefs" of "a customer franchise or constituency," a brand story that rests on a highly emotional and associative set of qualities; in the company's words, something "essentially intangible and built on perceptions." If young adults are the target audience, they might be cultivated at, for example, promotional events at downtown New York bars, where free designer rum drinks are on offer; the selling strategy here is associating the brand with an atmosphere. When aimed at a youth market, brand equity is about creating a permanent, positive association with a product, an effect one marketer dubs "ever-cool."

Ever-cool is such a high priority that a rash of companies have been competing to get their goods embedded in video game story lines. In the game "Darkened Skye," Skye of Lynlora fights the evil Lord Neccroft and his minions with rainbow-colored candy Skittles. In "Croc 2," the eponymous loveable outcast crocodile, a creature with loathsomely cute bad grammar, must buy LifeSavers Gummi Savers if he wishes to make special jumps—the advertising ploy gives a new literal meaning to "sugar high." Meanwhile, the bananas in "Super Monkey Ball" are tagged with Dole Food Company stickers. The lighters in "Die Hard: Nakatomi Plaza" are Zippos, and the cell phones are Motorola two-way radios. The cabs in "Crazy Taxi" go to Kentucky Fried Chicken and the surfers in "Surf Riders" wear G-Shock watches and use Mr. Zog's Sex Wax. The star of the sci-fi combat game "Wipeout XL" shares the screen with an ad for the brew Red Bull, although the drink has about as much to do with sci-fi warfare as teenybopper crooner Aaron Carter.

Lodging products in video game story lines is not an original idea. It comes, ironically enough, from network television, the media that video games are swiftly supplanting. In the "golden age" of television, adult programs had names such as *Camel News Caravan* and *Texaco Star Theater*; these shows benefited advertisers by having actor-shills sell their products directly to the audience. Strategic product tie-ins gave rise to a $200 million industry of toys and clothing based on licensed television characters such as Davey Crockett and Daniel Boone. As television historian Lawrence R. Samuels points out in his book *Brought to You By*, NBC's kids' show *The Magic Clown,* which debuted in 1949, cast Bonomo's Turkish Taffy as an intrinsic part of the plot.

Video game makers now deploy their television ancestors' aggressive but still covert sales tactics. In "Darkened Skye," Skittles have been cast as symbols rather than just sweets. They are, of all things, the sign of free expression: The mystical land's evil lord has decreed that all be dank and monochromatic, but the colorful candies are the tools of freedom that help bring a full palette back to the world. While chasing baddies in the fields, the heroine gathers orange Skittles descended from the heavens and uses them to cast magic spells. The game even quotes Skittles television commercials, and does so with the reverence an art filmmaker might show in quoting Vermeer. In "Darkened Skye," Skittles have an effect the opposite to the one they have in real life, in which their contribution is more along the lines of tooth decay and even early obesity.

SKATING ALL THE
WAY TO THE BANK

Given that "Pro Skater 3" is an extreme sports action game, it must at least appear to accord with the extreme sports value system, a complicated admixture of commercialism and refusal. I ask adult skaters, men in their twenties, whether they think the game succeeds on that front. One tells me that only certain brands are appropriate to promote in a skate-based video game (or skate event, for that matter). Real skater brands such as Airwalk and Vans are cool; Mountain Dew isn't, because it isn't "supporting the skate industry directly," an older skater informs me. A company that doesn't directly make skateboarding equipment isn't good, another explains, because when "the skateboard market shrinks, those other brands will disappear."

Brian Livov, twenty-nine, a swarthy, sturdily built older skater with intense black eyes, recalls that when he started skating seventeen years ago he had two skate shirts that he wore over and over again—they were all he could afford. He speaks resentfully about how skating has gone from "garage companies to multinationals," the latter who will presumably divest in skating the second it falls out of favor. "The younger skateboarders are all about brands, videos, and the Internet. They are programmed to buy," he says. "They want to show us their skater footage and the first thing they ask me when they see how good I am is, 'Are you sponsored?' That's their main goal now, it's what's sold to them. The game is part of the problem—brands like Birdhouse and DC [which make shoes, apparel, and boots] are way too extreme and commercial, you know?"

Dividing the world up into the smooth skater businessman of today and "the scumbag" of yesteryear, Livov shook an old edition of the skate magazine *Thrasher* at me and pointed out an ad for one of the few of today's skater-oriented brands he deems acceptable. The ad was for the company Consolidated Skateboards: "Don't you hate it when one of your favorite rides gets endorsed by a company you don't like or isn't even a skateboard company?" reads the ad. "These non-skateboarding companies see that skateboarding is getting popular and they want a piece of the action. . . . So What Do You Do??!!! Just don't buy their products. . . . These companies know that lots of skateboarders already know this, so they try to hide really good, with different names and separate warehouses."

According to the hypercritical skaters, many of the brands in the Tony Hawk game are inappropriate: Chrysler because it makes the familial minivans, of course, and Quiksilver because it's predominantly a surf brand. And the older skaters who resent the inescapable commercialism and assimilation of skate culture, are in fact, representative of a larger tendency within the sport. As Iain Borden writes in *Skateboarding, Space and the City,* skaters tend to endorse a "separate circuit of capital which exists entirely within skaters, skaters buying from other skaters," while remaining suspicious of the big cheesy companies that try to home in on the skaters' world.

Skateboarding has long contained commercial inclinations as well as a fierce anticorporate strain. The sport's beginnings were frankly commercial—skateboarding was a children's fad in the 1960s—but in the 1970s, it was reborn as a suburban kid's idea of a protest movement. Skaters were young teen hellions, latchkey kids who turned to skating from surfing and made their boards with their own hands. In 1975, a California drought produced empty swimming pools, and in those pools these ex-surfer urchins performed a stunning array of tricks never before seen.

These boys were soon tapped by marketers. The kids had a knack for selling magazines, boards, and clothing. Soon, you had Pepsi sponsoring a skate team, in 1977. Still, skaters defined themselves as antiestablishment, and the notion of skating as a resistant activity is still crucial to the sport. Kids who consider themselves "real" skaters say their sport is not about sportswear, but about expression and transgression. That's why it has always been important to skaters to ride where they're not wanted, and in particular to treat private space as public. As Borden writes, "Managers and owners of abstract space wish that society was solely directed at commodity production, exchange and consumption" and that skaters "refuse to engage in such processes." Skaters redefine business and governmental spaces as nonprofit places for imagination, athleticism, fun, and wandering.

But despite this mythology, skaters are also the most available peer-to-peer marketers around. They aspire to be on skateboard flow teams or, even better, obtaining the higher level of a sponsored amateur team; this way, they get free wheels and other gear from companies so that they can parade the stuff around their respective skate parks before anyone else can do the same.

Most kids will say they will do anything to be sponsored. Having a tony brand on his clothes or board seals a young skater's coolness and gives him, in the same way as it gives the regular teen trendspotter, a sense of being *near* both a celebrity skater and the brand that the celebrity skater is identified with. The members of flow teams, by the transitive property, imagine themselves to be stars through proximity to "important" brands.

Serious skaters are not the major force behind the rise of the Tony Hawk games—the three editions have sold too many copies for the audience not to be broad and general. But the Tony Hawk games have a lot to do with the rising status of the sport and through them many a teen and preteen knows all about the brands and the tricks. And the games are a tremendous selling device, for an obvious reason: if Pro Skater is your game, what else would you wear, in these intensely branded times, but skate clothes?

"Nowadays, you don't have to be a skater to look like a skater," says Jake Phelps, editor-in-chief of the skate magazine *Thrasher.* His view is that "Madison Avenue will jump on any of those trends that come down the pike," and that today's skaters are younger than ever, many starting at age eight, another example of the premature aging of the preteen market. Companies that rose out of the skateboard community have consolidated. Vans skate parks are part of larger malls, and Vans boutiques operate on these parks' premises. Skateboards and skateboard-related products from about 300 manufacturers of professional-level equipment generate $1.4 billion in annual retail sales. Clearly, all that can't be coming only from kids who actually skate.

Activision launched their extreme games in 1999, after noting the burgeoning participation rates in mountain biking, surfing, skateboarding, and anything else off the mainstream and at least fairly dangerous. (One of the most extreme of the cross-branded extreme sports games emerged in 2002, only it wasn't a video game, it was the film *XXX* that copped all the moves and the style of the video games.) The majority of the participants in those sports were between twelve and twenty-four—a perfect demographic. The gamers who now play "Tony Hawk" are typically not skaters first; they may get on boards after they have learned about ollies or toe grabs from their PlayStations. Because they usually fail miserably with their real bodies, they just increase their devotion to stars such as Hawk. "Hawk is a champion skater, he's marketing and merchandising, he's cashing in with the video games," explains *Thrasher*'s Phelps. "All the others have sold out to Larry Flynt and Time Warner anyway [referring to the magazine *Big Brother,* owned by Flynt]. And it's windfall for us [*Thrasher*] as well."

"The video game has made skating less subterranean," says skater Mark Hermoso. "Real skaters don't like how big it has gotten, how it's more about sponsors than having fun."

VIDEO GAME VERITE

Toward the end of 2002, product placement in video games intensified. Electronic Arts announced contracts equaling over $2 million integrating McDonald's and Intel products into "The Sims Online," with that terribly popular game's virtual characters dining on Mickey D fries and Big Macs, while booting up and tapping away on Intels, of course. The aim was to have the figures on screen actually use products rather than to have them merely flash past in a skateboard arena. Also in 2002 characters in the latest iteration of Kelly Slater's Pro Surfer game were revealed to be users of Nokia mobile phones (one assumes they stopped short of having the Nokia insignia bobbing on a crashing wave because it would have been too disconcerting.)

"What appeals to me most about product placement is not just shaking down the consumer," says Mike Fischer, Vice President of Entertainment Marketing at Sega. (Sega was the company that put the Dole stickers on the monkey's bananas in the Japanese version of "Super Monkey III.")

The Dole-stickered bananas, he says, "make the game more tangible." What they offer the companies who either buy into the game or make low- or high-level co-promoting deals with the games they have cross-marketed with (Sprite puts the game Street Hoops on 40 million containers of the soda: Street Hoops contains buses emblazoned with Sprite that ride by as virtual players shoot hoops in return.), says Fischer, is relevance. Relevance to the desirable, sometimes diffident teen male, mostly.

Fischer, like others in the video game industry, makes the argument that consumerism is real and therefore, for simulations to be "real," "true," and "authentic," they must contain logos. "Sure, you wouldn't expect to see a Domino's pizza product placement in *The Godfather*," Fischer explains, unwittingly positing a high-art, low-art theory about realism, "It has to be about staying true to the game. And branding is universal. Brands in video games are about finding an emotional connection and creating legitimacy for a brand or a partner."

The entity that gets video product placement right, he says, is the army, as in the game Operation Defend Freedom, with its American Army logo.

His is an aesthetic of resemblance, that rests on reproduction of the signs of money and exchange and logos is again as a stand-in for authenticity.

Game manufacturers' typical justifications for the new wave of video-game product placement are, strangely enough, aesthetic. Fischer himself explained the growth of the practice in an interview in 2001: "You don't pick up a facial tissue, you pick up a Kleenex. You don't pick up a corn chip, you pick up a Frito or a Dorito. In the video game experience, you don't want to drive to the fried chicken restaurant, you want to drive to KFC."

"When you get brands in front of teens through one of our extreme sports games, they are authentic, and help to create a more realistic fantasy," says Will Kassoy of Activision. "This is about authenticity. Tony Hawk wouldn't allow us to sell Visa in the game; we only brand with clothes and other items that are true to skateboarders."

A representative at Tony Hawk, Inc., Tony Hawk's managing and licencing firm, also describes Hawk's taste world in terms of a truth value with Hawk's choice of products to endorse deriving from what "is most authentic to the sport." While Hawk himself doesn't decide which products are included in the video game (although Quiksilver now happens to own Hawk's clothing line), he does have a group of endorsees ranging from Quicksilver to Bagel Bites to Arnette sunglasses. These are deemed authentic, explains the representative, because Hawk actually uses them.

The use of the term *authenticity* seems to be a sophisticated preemptive strike against a consumer rights critique of video game branding. The branded version of the world that is now invading kids' consciousness through their GameCubes is a strategic reproduction of a corporatized landscape, not an attempt at realness. The game manufacturers are relying on this canny equation in which copying the branded world is the same as authenticity. Of course, authenticity, if it exists at all, is more of a moral category than a mirror of the world. As Lionel Trilling wrote thirty years ago, authenticity is an even more "strenuous moral experience" than sincerity.

But placing products into video games and ensuring kids endless viewing has nothing to do with sincerity. Games, like so many other products, aim to harness teens' desire for an ideal—a "true" world—and give them a branded one instead.

PART TWO
self-branding

8

Body Branding:
Cosmetic Surgery

Carolyn, five feet two and 135 pounds, has blue eyes and platinum blonde hair. She lives in a wealthy suburb in the Mid West where kids with new money show it off by going to the salon regularly and being concerned about who made their pants and how much their jackets cost. Carolyn is like them in that she wears only posh brands such as Bebe and BCBG. Unlike her classmates, however, she lives modestly, with her divorced mother, a paralegal, in a two-story home; she works fifteen hours a week at a local upscale bakery so that she can buy her fancy clothes.

Carolyn is like many other middle-class teenagers today. But she is not like middle-class teenagers of a decade ago. Sure, she wants designer threads and, eventually, law school. What sets her apart from her teen predecessors is her most expensive dream: larger breasts. She has been obsessed with getting them since she was sixteen. Since then, not a day has gone by that she has not thought about her new, bigger breasts. She is ready to buy them the month she graduates from high school. Like other girls in her school who talk about plastic surgery nonstop, she says, she is getting her enlarged mammary glands as a graduation present; the only difference is that she is giving the present to herself.

So for six months Carolyn has been consulting a surgeon and keeping a booklet of her fears and questions. Will they be too hard or look like grapefruit halves? Will they lose feeling? These worries, and the health risks associated with surgery, aren't enough to dissuade her. "I want breast implants as soon as possible," she says.

Carolyn is not alone. In only one year, from 2000 to 2001, the number of cosmetic surgeries on teens eighteen and under has jumped 21.8 percent, from 65,231 to 79,501. Almost 306,000 of the 7.4 million plastic surgeries performed in 2000 in the United Sates were alterations of teens and children. In 2000, according to the American Society of Plastic Surgeons (ASPS), breast augmentation was the third most popular surgery for people eighteen and under, when 3,682 girls underwent the surgery. The same year, 29,700 teen noses were reshaped, 23,000 teen ears were done, 95,097 teens were chemically peeled, another 74,154 young faces were microdermabraded, and 45,264 kids had hair removed by laser. It should be noted that while saline breast implants are approved by the Food and Drug Administration only for women eighteen years or older, it is not illegal for doctors to perform implant surgery on minors, nor is it difficult for minors to find doctors who will do the procedure.

Minors need only find a particularly permissive and accommodating doctor—and there are many—who might find their physical "imperfection" worthy of a "medical" procedure as opposed to a merely cosmetic one. Once they have found a willing surgeon, the kids have their parents sign consent forms for surgery to be performed. As Paul Weiss, M.D., a member of the ASPS, puts it, "A girl ought to have the right to decide whether she wants breast implants if she is an otherwise normal sixteen-year-old with little breast development." Other situations include those where one breast develops normally, says Weiss, and the other doesn't much or one breast is normal size and the other is very large. As for liposuction, Weiss says that "teenagers are small adults, with a small difference in their physiology: hypothetically, if I saw a sixteen-year-old with normal body habitus but extremely heavy thighs, I wouldn't turn my nose up at liposuction."

Teenagers now alter their bodies extremely and proudly. Among teens eighteen and under in 1994, only 392 had breast augmentations and 511 liposuction; in 2001 there were 2,596 augmentations and 2,755 liposuctions among that age group, a 562 percent increase. According to the ASPS, the rate of liposuction and breast augmentation for all age groups increased by 386 percent and 476 percent respectively between 1992 and 2000.

"It's totally common for people to have their eyes done, their chins implanted, their ears pinned back," says Mara, a seventeen-year-old swan of a girl from Miami Beach. Mara is now a freshman at a New York City women's college. She still bears the markings of her palmy origins: the heavy makeup, the half-head of blonde highlights, the superthin frame, the tight designer pants and designer clutch handbag. "My friend went to Argentina for the summer and got surgery done—it's cheaper there," Mara explains. "What can you say? Plastic surgery is more and more accepted, and people do it either in fifth grade or after high school, before college."

For Mara, and for the teens who now get plastic surgery, the procedures themselves are not a cause for shame. The real cause of embarrassment is having one's peers notice the change in appearance. That's why Jessica notes that the best time for the alteration is between middle school and junior high, junior high or high school, or high school and college, to lessen the chances of that sort of chagrin.

Manhattan-based facial plastic surgeon Phillip Miller, M.D., says that 30 percent of his practice consists of teens who get smaller noses or bigger lips—"luscious" mouths, in the argot of the beauty magazines. The plumping effect is produced through injections of collagen (good for five months) or by the permanent implants of fat that has been removed from other parts of the body. The girls present Miller with displays of fashion models from *Mademoiselle, Cosmo, Elle,* and *Allure,* and pictures of lippy movie stars such as Angelina Jolie and Julia Roberts. These women have lips that "make teens self-aware of what they may not have," as Miller puts it.

Growing up in a social context in which models' bodies are used to sell products and lifestyles and atmospheres, teenagers feel significant pressure to purchase whatever it takes to become part of that role. This takes a psychic toll on Generation Y, and a financial one as well. To buy her $7,000 breast implants, Carolyn will spend part of a $100-a-week allowance, along with the money she makes at her job. Her aunt will throw in $2,000. The final $1,000 will be put on Carolyn's credit card, making her part of a new legion of teenagers carrying credit card debt. (According to Nellie Mae, students owed an average of $2,327 in credit card debt in 2001.)

The teenagers who now seek surgery can't imagine a time when there wasn't so much media coverage and salesmanship of these bodily correctives. When I speak to them, I remember my own adolescence, before the self-branding of the teen body really took. In 1985, at age thirteen, I, too, experienced intense physical self-loathing. I hid my mortifying "womanly" breasts under oversized boys' clothing because I hated them and what they meant. With the assurance that nothing could be done, I transformed this self-hatred into a hipster androgyny and became a creature of the mind—mostly a creature of my own mind. Perhaps this wasn't the best way. But at least when I and others like me left that visceral self-disgust behind at about sixteen, when we became happier in our own skins, our transformation was a result of character development and improving mental health, not a newly puffy mouth or surgically inflated breasts.

But it is different in the age of public flesh. If I were a teen today, I'm sure I would also be goaded by "abvertisements" (or ads that use sinewy abdomens to sell) in the magazines and would feel the urge to trawl the Web for beauty remedies. As so many girls do now, I might also trade my clumsy, inverted bookishness, body obscured under a plaid shirt that smells like patchouli and dust, and hair hanging blackly over my eyes for what would appear on the surface to be radiant, adult sexuality.

Julie, now a sweet-voiced, well-grounded business student of twenty-one, recalls the thinking that finally led her to get a $6,800 nose job. Growing up in North Hollywood, she recalls, she noticed girls in magazines with their perfect bodies and perfect facial features, and she became acutely aware of her flaws. "There are all these perfect things all around and you realize you don't look like that. In all the advertisements, there are no fat girls, no big-nosed girls," she says. "When I was younger, all the movie stars had surgery, which was comforting—all those people did it, went through it, why can't I?" she adds, her recognition that these stars used artificial means to achieve perfection consoling her that such alterations are both possible and commonplace enough among the celebrity class not to seem dangerous for an ordinary person. Julie then says that it became even more reasonable to her when "almost anyone" started to get nose jobs—the procedure seemed less vain and iconoclastic.

For Generation Y, liposuction is not just for Bel Air television producers' daughters but also for eighteen-year-old shop girls in Yonkers. First the province of the syphilitic and deformed, then of theater and movie stars, then of the rich, plastic surgery has become naturalized for the upper- and lower-middle classes.

In fact, Dr. Miller says he sees teens drawn to what he thinks is the remaining luxurious stigma of plastic surgery, the I-can't-believe-I-am-in-a-plastic surgeon's office frisson that excites both the young patient and the patient's parent. Like the other markers of affluence among an American middle class still anxious about its social position, a self-bettering beauty treatment is some proof that a girl has made it to the upper echelons, that her family no longer has necessities, only stylized tastes and desires. The sociologist Pierre Bourdieu has written that as the distance from necessity grows, some then mark this distance by "proving" their superiority to those who are ruled by needs, not wants. The girls who have plastic surgery use their improved bodies as proof of their supremacy to those who simply survive as they live out their days in fat, small-breasted, ordinary bodies that are destined more for laboring than for shopping.

Sociology aside, could the trend in youthful plastic surgery continue without an increase in advertising? Not likely. In fact, it was an antitrust court decision in the 1970s that deregulated medical advertising and ads for learned professional service. That decision cleared the way for the barrage of ads for the surgery we see today.

Slowly but inexorably, doctors began to advertise. As Deborah Sullivan writes in *Cosmetic Surgery: The Cutting Edge of Commercial Medicine in America,* there was a time when a plastic surgeon with a license plate that read "BOOBS" was state-of-the-art advertising for the industry. It took a decade for the paid ads for plastic surgery that appeared in the late 1970s to suffuse the backs of magazines, newspapers, and the yellow pages, all promising larger, firmer breasts, flatter tummies, tinier noses, stronger jaws. For today's teenagers, "breast augmentation" and "liposuction" are literally household words.

Still, it is the editorial media coverage of cosmetic surgery that really lures consumers, including teens. Plastic surgeons now pay up to $6,000 monthly to public relations representatives to ensure a client base. The fruits of these PR firms' labors are the stories appearing in women's magazines that showcase plastic surgery. In the 1960s, a scant 15 articles about plastic surgery appeared in the major women's magazines listed in the *Reader's Guide to Periodical Literature*. In the 1970s, the number rose to 55. In the 1980s, it nearly doubled to 107. Since the later 1980s, there has been a general rise in stories about breast augmentations—countless newspaper articles and television shows and even stories in general-interest magazines—and the *Reader's Guide* listed 39 articles on plastic surgery in the bigger women's magazines in 1999 alone. "Commercialism," Sullivan writes, "like Pandora's box, is full of problems for the medical profession's service ethic, occupational authority and autonomy."

Cosmetic surgeons and their new publicists are simply joining in the aggressive branding that has long characterized the industries competing for beauty consumers' dollars. And compete they do; if there was a time when doctors tried to maintain a special dignity in their marketing, that time has passed. On their Web sites, surgeons play ruthlessly on teenagers' desire for relief from their self-contempt. The Web site of Barry Davidson, M.D., for instance, offers up the profile of a fifteen-year-old as an inspiration to other girls with "weak" chins and "hook" noses. Incidentally, the ad copy echoes Jessica's thought on the timing of teen surgeries: "This patient elected to undergo rhinoplasty and chin implant during the summer vacation between high school and college," it reads. "This is a choice that is often made so that no explanations will be required to her new classmates."

Other cosmetic surgery sites are more subtle, but no less assured in their marketing agenda. While striking a temperate, caring medical stance—asking the potential clients seeking nose jobs about their emotional readiness, for example—they all the while note that new noses and chins boost "self-esteem" in the very young. The site of one cosmetic surgeon exhorts parents to "discuss with your teenager why he or she may feel insecure" and follows up with a promise of psychic happiness resulting from going under the knife: "One teenager suffered years of acne and was left with extensive scarring," it reads. "After he and his parents pursued scar revision surgery, the teen expressed that his biggest joy was not being teased about the scarring like he had been teased about the acne. Teens who pursue facial plastic or reconstructive surgery are looking to feel more confident and have a better self-image." Perhaps the most overt and unbecoming plea for teen beauty dollars appears on a surgery site that claims "successful plastic surgery may result in reversal of the social withdrawal that so often accompanies teens who feel 'different.'"

The teen breast augmentation fetish has also been egged on by other advertisements in magazines such as *Teen Vogue* and *Seventeen*. The two mags have run ads (the ads were full-page in *Teen Vogue*) for Bloussant, an herbal breast enhancement tablet. Bloussant is, like all herbal supplements, unregulated by the FDA and costs $229 for an eight-week supply. The results are dubious at best, but these magazines—which have the trust of preteens and young teenagers—have carried advertisements for Bloussant, mixed in with the usual stories about boyfriends and makeup tips. The photo in the ad is of an ample young woman dripping out of her bathing suit; the text promises a "less invasive alternative to cosmetic surgery" resulting in increased cleavage, firmness, and fullness. *Seventeen* has unapologetically run the ad at least three times.

Perhaps it's no coincidence that in an October 2000 *Seventeen* magazine questionnaire of readers from thirteen to twenty-two years old found that 25 percent had considered liposuction, tummy tucks, or breast augmentation, while 12 percent had considered nose jobs.

Some of the purveyors of these beauty fantasies, the plastic surgeons, don't seem money-mad at first blush, but rather sober and kindly. Nevertheless, they work from the assumption that for their patients, happiness will happen through physical correction toward a normative mean. When I meet with a genial New York-based plastic surgeon named Brian Forley, M.D., for example, he tells me the story of how he augmented the breast of a fifteen-year-old with an asymmetrical bosom: "The girl limited her social engagements because of her deformity [the smaller breast]," he says. "She was looking for a way out. I found it medically appropriate to reconstruct."

Forley doesn't question why a girl with one smaller breast might consider the asymmetry a deformity, which seemed to me arguable. But it's common now for teenagers to consider lumpy thighs, a fleshy midriff, or small breasts to be horrific aberrations. Such is the price of viewing one too many teen catalog models. They imagine that becoming perfect will make them more and more socially acceptable. Obviously, that's the impulse behind the thousands and thousands of nose jobs teens have subjected themselves to over the past three decades.

Breast augmentation, on the other hand, speaks to a different and very current impulse—the desire to redesign oneself into a being that one's social group agrees is sexualized. Girls who get breast augmentation are more interested in sexualizing themselves than merely "normalizing" their faces. Teen girls who get the breast enhancements wish to be erotic objects of consumption, following the not-so-hidden currents in the general culture that both eroticizes teenage girls and punishes those who act on their libidinal impulses. On a teen Internet chat line, a girl writes that she wants breast augmentation because her 34B breasts are "a little on the saggy side." She adds, "I'd like them to be perky and fuller. The cost isn't an issue," her mind full of images of such "perfect" breasts from films and magazines, these breasts acting as a tacit competitor with her for sexual supremacy in social situations.

HAPPINESS
THROUGH THE BEAUTIFUL

That achieving physical normalcy or aesthetic perfection will bring about happiness is not a new idea. According to historian Joan Jacobs Brumberg, author of the *The Body Project: An Intimate History of American Girls,* Victorian-era girls were also taught to be most interested in their bodies. Their interests, however, followed different contours. Those girls were corseted and virginal at all costs, while their contemporary versions may starve, work out, wax, pierce, and tattoo their bodies, but nonchalantly relinquish their virginity.

But Brumberg also writes that girls today are much more bodily oriented. Nineteenth-century young women "had a very different orientation from those of girls today. . . . [before World War I] girls rarely mentioned their bodies in terms of strategies for self-improvement." In contrast, in this age of branded youth, the body is regarded as something to be processed, plucked, and subdued, refined through financial expenditure.

Sander Gilman, in his 1998 book *Creating Beauty to Cure the Soul: Race and Psychology in the Shaping of Aesthetic Surgery,* links the growth of cosmetic surgery to the relatively new prevalence of Prozac and an increased medicalization of psychological pain: If one kind of individual happiness is achievable through external medical means and is worth the price, by the same logic a saline intervention on a miserable and small-breasted girl may be just as worthwhile. "The idea of the cure of the psyche as central to the undertaking of aesthetic surgery postulates a 'patient' with a 'healthy' body but an 'unhappy soul,'" as Gilman puts it.

And like shopping at high-rent venues, this faith in surgical beautification and the consumption of luxury goods is often transmitted from parents to children as well. Both mothers and daughters may now view their bodies as plastic, moldable objects, constructed according to one's own will: All it takes to transform a mind or body is the money with which to purchase a new one. As the *Boston Globe* put it in March 2001, baby boomer enthusiasm has spilled over to other generations: "Many cosmetic surgeons say their teenage clientele has increased significantly in recent years. . . . Former patients transmit tips about surgery and surgeons to their children in a modern rite of passage. [Barry] Davidson [a plastic surgeon] says he routinely sees two generations of breast implants, and three generations is not uncommon. 'A daughter with the same build as her mother and grandmother sees what they had done and decides she can do something about it, too,' he explains."

The numbers confirm that Generation Y's parents are also getting surgery in record numbers; in 2000, 3.2 million people between the ages of thirty-five and fifty had cosmetic plastic surgery. Cosmetic surgery has become so commonplace that it has come to resemble the rest of the designer products mothers and daughters share.

Phillip Miller also sees a new acceptance of plastic surgery within families. "The mother had rhinoplasties at sixteen and seventeen," says Miller of the adolescent surgeries of thirty or so years ago, a more secretive practice that was more often tied up with a desire to assimilate out of one's ethnicity. "When they bring their daughters in for them, they feel camaraderie with their children," he says. "They say proudly, 'Now my daughters are getting it.'" A darker version of this scenario occurs, as well. "If the mother didn't have one, she may feel a little jealous—she wanted one as a child," says Miller. "By and large, these mothers also feel excitement that their daughters are getting something they couldn't have or afford for themselves when they were teenagers."

Carolyn grew up as part of this culture, seeing the upper-middle-class moms in their thirties, forties, and fifties with bust implants. These mothers, she says, offer them to their daughters. (Or are themselves plastic surgeons: the doctor who will operate on Carolyn is the father of a kid at her school.)

And affluent parents who refuse their children's requests for surgery no longer necessarily speak from a position of certitude or strength. They may be so confused and ambivalent about their daughters' pleas that they need the plastic surgeon not for the surgery itself but for the reinforcement in their efforts to discourage their daughters from going under the knife. With a sort of morose nonchalance, plastic surgeon Brian Forley tells me about the mothers who have visited his office with their daughters. When one sixteen-year-old girl visited him in tears and told him that she just had to have new breasts, her mother sat and listened, her face frozen. Forley conjectures that the parent thought of him as the last resort. "She hoped I would talk some sense into her daughter," he said. "I tried." (Of course, not all plastic surgeons try to dissuade young girls from nonmedical surgeries; it's likely that the girl would find someone else do the surgery if one plastic surgeon wouldn't.)

Given the social climate, it is not surprising that Forley's patient did not come by her common sense on her own; she is, after all, very young. The branding of the flesh starts earlier than ever before, in the tween years. As one sixteen-year-old recently said before her breast augmentation surgery, "I was probably about thirteen when I started, you know, considering having surgery to correct my breasts."

Carolyn began to dream about larger breasts at that same age. "As long as I can remember, I never liked my breasts," she says. "Since I was thirteen, I was insecure when I was getting intimate with someone—I just don't like my body. I wanted augmentation when I was thirteen, and that was even before I had access to nude photos."

We may worry about these children's dented self-images and precocious, other-focused sexuality, but the truth of the matter is that our social order has created the double bind. Girls and women are actively encouraged to resemble the processed goods they consume. They wish to buy and then to become the perfect profiles of the media stars and movie heroines who are now themselves surgically altered and enhanced. They also dwell in the "after" side of the "before" and "after" surgical narrative, inspired by this primitive advertising technique or laudatory nonfiction accounts of the procedure. As Carolyn says, "I was watching something on HBO about a plastic surgery and decided to go for it."

Fake décolletage everywhere has an insalubrious effect on teenagers. One could argue that the manufacturing of this inadequacy is a sales strategy—a superior one, for it opens the door for the suggestion that the adolescent's physical inadequacy can be remedied by a purchase, be it thongs, jeans, or augmentation. (One plastic surgeon comments that teens now treat cosmetic alterations as if they were designer jeans.) It was the rumors of Britney Spears' breast implant surgery, doctors say, that spurred the latest and most intense interest in breast implant surgery among the very young. The girls who self-brand through plastic surgery do mention Spears and other media avatars of voluptuousness, such as actress Halle Berry.

Such ample women are also more likely to appear nearly undressed in public, revealing all their natural or newly acquired charms. Today's adolescents are surrounded by more exposed flesh than girls of previous generations, especially from the quasi-pornography of the laddie magazines *Maxim, FHM,* and *Gear.* Those magazines, no longer relegated to the pornographic brown wrappers of yore, display teen starlet cover girls, complete with their prerequisite, unnaturally firm bosoms, who smile meretriciously down at American girls from the windows of all magazine stores. None of these magazines existed a decade ago. Music videos have had a similar effect.

"Teenagers are more cognizant of the size of their breasts due to music videos," asserts Forley. "Prior to the expansion of MTV, girls had far less access to such constant imagery. Now they see them everywhere and they believe large breasts are the norm."

America's love affair with gigantism, the philosophy that bigger is better, also plays a role in the new surgeries. Carolyn compares it with a giggle to supersizing. She says her desire for implants is similar to her taste for acrylic nails "that are longer and longer, so long they are ghetto fabulous." (She refers to the extremely long, often decorated talons preferred by some African American teenagers.) "I start with three-inch stiletto heels and I go to five-inch ones," she adds. "The desire for more and bigger just hits me all of a sudden."

The comparison is flip and Carolyn knows it. But she's not entirely kidding. Carolyn and the thousands of other girls getting implants have grown up watching giant films and their even more gargantuan sequels. They have played in theme parks that go on forever. They have eaten enormous bags of chips and great buckets of movie popcorn. Supersizing means that a Coca-Cola at Burger King now runs as big as 42 ounces, and a large order of French fries is double the size it was a few years ago. It's no wonder that kids are supersized, too: Obesity engulfs 17 percent of the teen population, a number they have grown into from kids and preteens—where one child in seven is obese. Today's generation of rampant teenage consumers have lived only in the era of supersizing; they know no other. They cannot distinguish the proper size of breasts, bank accounts, or cola portions.

Teens and tweens are perhaps more open to altering or branding their bodies than adults. The idea of a permanent change to the body—made practically overnight—appeals to adolescents, people who are by definition shifting identity daily. The more expensive, so much the better. Many teenage cosmetic surgeries emanate from self-aversion, camouflaged as an emblem of self-esteem and normalcy. The girl who chooses cosmetic surgery chooses obsession with the body and mastery over it rather than an attempt at the transcendence that means forgetting the body.

"Implants will make me much more confident," Carolyn says, not terribly convincingly. "Once I get them I will get used to them, and they will change the distorted perception of how my body is."

9

X-Large and X-Small

"Supersize your superset" proclaims one teen weightlifter, echoing female teens' urges to augment their breasts.

The term *superset* refers to an extraordinary number of exercises, or weightlifting sets, performed with little or no rest between them. The hope for the boys who do supersets is to grow big—bigger than their classmates, as big as male models, professional wrestlers, and bodybuilders. In a sense, teen superset obsessions result from branding efforts as well—the selling of nutritional-supplement companies and preppy clothing manufacturers such as Abercrombie & Fitch. In just five years, these firms have created a greater sense of inadequacy among boys about their bodies than ever before. Not so coincidentally, this has produced a whole new market for underwear and powdered drinks that teen boys now buy in an attempt to end this inadequacy. An astronomical and younger-than-ever use of steroids accompanies it all, along with a trade in dubious, over-the-counter nutritional supplements. The drive to grow big, like the drive for youthful plastic surgery, goes beyond becoming big or becoming perfect; it's the sort of self-construction that Generation Y understands. It's self-branding as an emotional palliative.

According to a Blue Cross-Blue Shield 2001 survey of ten-to-seventeen-year-olds, half of the 785 children interviewed said they were "aware" of sports supplements and drugs, and one in five take them. Forty-two percent did it to build muscle and 16 percent just to look better (i.e., "built"). These numbers are way up: In contrast, the 1999 BCBS survey found that no sample of kids under fourteen had taken products.

The push began in 1999 with the emergence of products such as Teen Advantage Creatine Serum, which made appearances on the shelves of vitamin chain stores. The marketing shows a kind of malignant genius: The formula was developed, according to the label, "especially for young aspiring athletes 8–19 years of age." (It also carries the necessary but misleadingly low-key caveat that excess dosage of creatine is not a "wise decision.") Not surprisingly, the products took off; there's nothing like a new teen-specific product that claims to alleviate a new teen-specific pathology.

The campaign worked so well that 52 percent of young users of performance-enhancing supplements said they had tried creatine (only 18 percent of adults surveyed used these supplements). Other supplements popular with kids—kids as young as ten—include ephedrine (which ostensibly increases endurance) and "andro," or androstenedione, an over-the-counter alternative to anabolic steroids (like steroids, androstenedione increases testosterone in the body—in fact, it also increases production of estrogen). These supplements, experts agree, range from suspect to dangerous, and even deadly, as ephedra turned out to be. In fact, some of these supplements, says Charles Yesalis, author of *The Steroids Game,* are permitted to be called supplements only because of legal loopholes and are in fact drugs that are virtually unregulated by the FDA.

All this supplement use does not, unfortunately, mean that kids are staying away from steroids: In the 2001 Monitoring the Future study, 2.8 percent of eighth graders, 3.5 percent of tenth graders, and 3.7 percent of twelfth graders said they had taken steroids, meaning they had "cycled" on the drugs from eight to twelve weeks at least once (only 1.7 percent of high school sophomores had taken steroids in 1992). Why? Because steroids change body fat by adding muscle and thus decrease body fat proportionally. The possible side effects of steroids include stunted bone growth, liver damage, and shrunken testicles. A cycle is also costly, ranging from a few hundred to a few thousand dollars. But, as happens with a new wardrobe or a new pair of breasts, that's not seen as much of a price for looking more attractive. Allowances are up, working hours are up; kids can afford to juice. In such an environment, the decision not to use steroids but to depend instead on supplements can seem both cautious and economical. The no-worries attitude toward supplements, and dependence on them, can be seen in Sam, a thoughtful, quiet, dedicated prep school sophomore. Sam is also a prize-winning sixteen-year-old bodybuilder who writes for teen bodybuilding sites on which he proudly posts photos of his rippling and massive physique. Every day, Sam takes ephedrine mixed with caffeine along with 5 milligrams of creatine. He's been lifting weights since he was seven, and his punishing regimen now takes two hours of lifting daily.

Sam's passion for weightlifting started when he was exploring a hotel where he was staying with his family and he saw an adult lifting in the weight room. This weightlifter was his version of Edgar Allen Poe's Annabel Lee—he would never forget the image of the strong older man lifting the barbells. As soon as he got home, he bought some weights at a discount store and began working on getting big. Sam is not alone in starting so early. It's a trend that echoes the other ways in which kids are getting older younger in the

market economy: Thirty-five percent of 60,000 weightlifting in-
juries in 1998 were for those aged from fifteen to twenty-four, and
12 percent were suffered by *children* aged from five to fourteen.

Today, he weighs 225 pounds, and has 6 percent body fat. He
says that lifting helps him "stay healthy, look good, and feel confident," but acknowledges that for some of his peers, "exposed to
weightlifting at first by popular culture" the reasons for their passions are not as hale and hearty. Some use steroids, for instance.
(His own practice of taking ephedrine—an herbal supplement that
can lead to heart attacks, seizures, psychoses, and death—to lose
weight is arguably not such a great way of "staying healthy" either.)
"There is definitely undue pressure on teen boys to look good and
be big," Sam says. There is also undue pressure not to be fat given
the commercial pressure to eat and the rising rates of obesity
spurred on by commercials for fattening and sugary foods. In the
stories of adolescents, childhood and teen obesity is a recurring
theme. "The fat child is more abused than the muscled one; look at
Piggy in *Lord of the Flies*," explains Sam. "The big boy with the
glasses—nobody listens to him. Teens now start lifting because they
are overweight."

For sure, teen male body culture is a response to the now ubiquitous overweight childhoods of American boys; a fat child may put
a hard body between the self that was ostracized and emasculated
flesh and his new adolescent self. The teen muscle boys, like the
breast augmentation girls, exchange one supersized consumerism
for another: They trade family-sized packages of branded food
bought in bulk at discount stores for giant, branded adult-male-
looking bodies and large vats of powdered supplements.

Juan, a Cuban American sixteen-year-old bodybuilder who lives
in New Jersey, used weightlifting to go from 225 pounds to 165
pounds in one year. He says he started weightlifting because he "got

a lot of prejudice" when he was fat. "That's why I did it [weightlifting], so they wouldn't make fun of me." Now his classmates respect him, he says, and girls talk to him, although he doesn't care about girls; he's more interested in the company of other high school weightlifters. "I want to get big, really big, but natural. I wanna be feared," Juan says. Like Sam, Juan doesn't consider the supplements unnatural—he takes from 5 to 10 milligrams of creatine a day, as well as whey for protein and glutamine for joint strength.

The desire of adolescents to leave behind the scrawny or husky teaseable boy for the hard, well-packaged man is not a new one, of course. The virtues of the well-developed man are extolled in the writings of the Greeks and in Shakespeare's *Measure for Measure:* "O, it is excellent / To have a giant's strength; but it is tyrannous / To use it like a giant." The wish to become big in puberty, for reasons of both dominance over one's peers and of display, can be seen in the twentieth century in the fifty years of Charles Atlas magazine advertisements. The Atlas ads famously promised pubescents bodybuilding courses that would "make you a new man in just 15 minutes a day," that could "'RE-BUILD' skinny rundown weaklings" into creatures with "a coat of muscle straight across your stomach." In addition, bodybuilding magazines aimed at boys have a long history (and so do complementary homoerotic physique magazines). The 1977 film *Pumping Iron* also gave encouragement to boys to build themselves up.

However, the omnipresent gymmed-out, almost-naked male body began to make the rounds only in the late 1980s. A big force for this was a new advertising culture—the giant billboards for Calvin Klein underwear flaunting well-built models, the denuded male torsos in that same designer's perfume ads, helped to change the shape of men, literally. It is no coincidence that this was a period when the teen members of Generation Y were toddlers.

"When you hear girls gawking at Abercrombie & Fitch about how hot the guy is on the bag—that makes an impression," one teen bodybuilder told the *New York Times Magazine* in 1999. One of Abercrombie's countless bare-chested and buff youths had clearly been seared on that teen's mind; perhaps he still thinks of him every time he makes yet another andro shake.

The rise of teen male bigoriexa, as media wags have called it, has also been spurred on by a new strain of magazines as well. There's the abdomen-mania of the men's magazines that these boys have grown up with, from *Men's Health* to *GQ*. In 2000, for instance, *Men's Heath* even launched a magazine in celebration of the teen male abdomen called *MH-17*. According to its initial press release, *MH-17* was "aimed at the 'rapidly growing' market of male teenagers in the United States."

MH-17 and its ideology of male teen "fitness" (read: male bodily self-hatred) flopped. But the tyranny of taut, ripped, and dieted teen male bodies on screen and in advertisements still rules. Teen films, for example, almost entirely lack the sloppy, scrawny, or plumpish boys of yesteryear, boys who were blissfully oblivious of the body obsession of their female counterparts. Now even those who play geeks, actors such as Jason Biggs of *American Pie 2,* are forced to have washboard stomachs or "six-packs" and to bare them constantly.

To achieve the required body, teen boys are willing to put in time and painful effort that many of their fathers couldn't have imagined—becoming a branded boy body takes just as much labor and pain as becoming a branded girl body. For instance, teen boy bodybuilders tend to engage in spartan, highly structured eating patterns. On the teenbodybuilder.com Web site, one boy describes the ten austere meals on his daily menu for the months when he prepares for competition. The meals are austere, obsessively observed, and protein-filled fare, one consisting of one scoop of egg white protein, one scoop of casein, half a scoop of Optimum's whey, four slices of turkey, and two pieces of whole wheat bread.

In their urge to build themselves into commercially approved hypermasculine specimens, the boys of Generation Y are in solidarity with their long-suffering female peers. Once there was a hope among feminists that girls could be taught to escape their oppressive body project. This has not occurred. Now, boys partake in it as well. Weightlifting, enthusiasts say, is a form of self-construction. For the teen weightlifters, however—boys shooting steroids and eating egg whites for breakfast; shaving their chests and backs and legs—the line between self-betterment and a morphic pathology is a blurry one.

THE PRO-ANA TEENS

"My name is Cheallaigh (pronounced Kelly)," reads the home page. "I have had anorexia for six years, of the bulimic subtype. I weigh 120 and I am 5'6". I am 17 and attending community college (see below). This page is my personal diary of my love affair with anorexia."

Cheallaigh is not using the word "love affair" lightly or ironically. She is truly besotten with anorexia and she is not alone: She is one of a new movement of girls, many of them teenagers, who dub themselves pro-anorexics. They dwell clandestinely on the Internet and chat about their starvation methods, their feelings, and, of course, their hatred of fatness. Those who produce their own pro-anorexic sites proffer "thinspiration" photographs of supermodels and tiny actresses—Shalom Harlow, Kate Moss, Gisele Bundchen, Calista Flockhart—often digitally altered to look even thinner. The authors of sites tend to give instructions to other girls like them; for example, chew ice, sit in rooms so cold that you shiver and thus burn calories, and never eat more than three hundred calories a day.

Although the minds behind these sites create collages and pastiches, they are not artists, unless you consider them hunger artists. They exist in chat rooms and on Web rings or circles of sites that link to one another. Like the girls branding their bodies through plastic surgery, the pro-ana teenagers trumpet their obsession and take it on as an identity. They showcase their starved frames on the Web in text or image rather than hide them, as anorexics typically do.

These girls were unwilling to meet with me face-to-face, but in July 2001 I communicated with them by phone or e-mail. That same month, the pro-anas were "discovered" by many magazines and newspapers, all of which devoured the girls' narratives, as it were. The *New York Post* blared "SICK WORLD OF PRO-ANOREXIA INTERNET SITES" while *USA TODAY* dubbed it "Super-thin, super-troubling."

By the end of the month, the pro-anas' macabre, emaciated zone was under attack. Their sites were summarily removed by Yahoo!, and they were widely condemned for encouraging self-starvation in other young women. At last check in 2002, the sites still existed all over the place but under non-Yahoo! domains. Their addresses, bearing such names as "No Curves," verged on self-parody. The most striking mark of all was the image of a badge on one pro-ana site. "We all need understanding," the site read, accompanied by a red ribbon and a new acronym, "E.D., End Discrimination Against Pro-Anorexics." It was an acronym whose economy and catchiness apotheosized pro-ana branding of the disease.

Who are they, these dark, self-branding teens? There was Jenny, fifteen, who lived in a New Jersey suburb, her hair a golden blonde, her clothes from Old Navy. "I think it's a bunch of girls who are struggling with who they are, and who they've become, and they try and find each other for support," Jenny wrote to me that summer. Another pro-ana girl, Vicki, also fifteen, testified that being anorexic gave her a stronger image of herself. "When you have goals set in front of you and when you know what you feel is 'good' or 'bad,' then you have self-confidence in yourself before you do it," said Vicki. "I look good, I feel good, I am good. It's about a large population of people seeing 'thin' as something beautiful."

Amanda, nineteen, recounted that *Cosmopolitan* gave her "thin-spiration." She said she looked down on girls who wore unfashionable clothes, and that she spent most of her money on makeup, clothes, and lingerie. "I don't think I could pinpoint one thing that makes me happy being an anorexic," she said. "I suppose it makes me feel special in a way, that it's something not everybody can have, and that I have more control over myself than anybody else."

The most plaintive response from the pro-anas was one I recognized personally. "It is disheartening to be faced with these extremely tall, thin, beautiful girls wherever you go," Linda told me. "The beauty can be explained away by 'it's all makeup,' height ignored, as there's nothing anyone can do about their height, but thinness is always seen as something you have control over. And if you could just be as thin as these women, then maybe you'd be as happy as they appear and just maybe instead of your guy looking at the billboard with lust they'll look at you that way."

I had experienced this feeling as an adolescent and young woman—that I was always second best to the celebrity or the girl with the virtues of a celebrity: heliotropism, self-possession, blonde-blue-eyed-ness. But contemporary girls like Linda are different from the eating disordered girls I knew at summer camp, high school, and in the freshmen college dorm. Those who suffered from the full-fledged disease fifteen years ago treated it as a private pathology. There was no Web community, no performance culture where a girl could boast of her sickness. I myself for two years didn't eat anything before dinner: I felt as Linda did. But there was no chance I would have wanted to share these feelings with anyone: God forbid that I identified myself as someone who would resort to such desperate and vain measures as *not eating.*

This is not true of the pro-ana. Like girls with fake breasts, like boys with sixteen-inch biceps, the pro-anas direct their efforts toward a single, highly orthodox standard, which they communicate to one another. They know beauty has a use and they are willing to say it. They are well-versed in physical fantasy.

This shift to an extreme willingness to announce one's attempt to inhabit a physical fantasy may well have a social explanation. The obsession with bigness and smallness has social class shadings and that such regard for and maintenance of beauty are the earmarks of the petit bourgeoisie rather than the working class. Ever-growing numbers of Americans and their children now believe they are middle class and subscribe to the conduct of that class, and I tend to think that this has speeded teens' mass internalization of the middle-class ideology that worships the perfected body. Pierre Bourdieu writes of middle-class French women in the 1970s, women who "devote such great investments of self-denial and especially of time, to improving their appearance, and are such unconditional believers in all forms of cosmetic voluntarism (plastic surgery)." This description applies to the adolescents who wish to improve themselves and shore up their new-found class identities through branding in their fashions and their bodies.

As I trolled the pro-ana Web sites, dominated by images of the wispy fashion models that the pro-anas idolize, it was hard not to recall the religious history of emaciation. The sites all bore quasi-religious names: "starve me sane"; "my goddess ana." Anorexia was originally a variety of sacral enthusiasm called *anorexia mirabilis:*

European religious women with the condition in the thirteenth and fourteenth centuries fasted to the point of having visions, going into frenzies in which they felt union with God and sometimes dying. Later, Protestant evangelicals engaged in pious starvation.

By the nineteenth-century, however, the consequences of fasting were considered a medical condition. The religious ascetic who starved his or her body was placed in an asylum, not glorified in a hagiography or on the cover of a magazine. As William James writes, "the general optimism and healthy-mindedness of liberal Protestant circles today makes mortification for mortification's sake repugnant to us."

In the 1870s, adolescent girls became "victims" of anorexia the disease, anorexia nervosa. Social historians have traced the rise in this adolescent syndrome to the emergence of the repressive, sentimental family, whose middle-class rites of caring and control centered around the evening meal and whose parenting rested on lovingly erasing the identities of their daughters.

The family-romance-as-wreck stands as one reading of anorexic girls. But in today's supersaturated zone of advertising images, another reading tends to go alongside the first: pro-anorexics are self-branders who have literally internalized an ad-mad world. And the pro-anas not only internalize these images but project them outwards, onto their Web sites, for all the world to see.

The dietetic ads started in the 1950s, as did teen magazine warnings that girls had better stay thin. But the pressure to be thin is worse now than ever before. Models are so slender that you can see every muscle—lean, toned, and sinewy—and this public flesh induces girls to compare every undressed part of these bodies to their own and then seek ceaselessly and impossibly to perfect their own bodies. It is in this climate that pro-anas have self-branded; instead of buying Tommy Hilfiger, they buy the idea of the tiny supermodel body clad in underwear and try to become her in the only way they know how. They appropriate the fashion images of the terribly disappearing media beauties that marketers haunt them with and then, in an inadvertent subversion, reveal these fashion models for what they really are: anorexic poster girls.

"With the Internet, it was bound to happen," one pro-ana explained of the photo collages on her site. "But rather than creating the movement, or even helping it along really, the pictures are just collected where they are easily accessed by millions to provide triggers." In a perverse sideline, the teenage pro-ana tribe actually took on the lingo of therapy directed at anorexics. They labeled the models' photos on their sites "trigger pictures," using a negative clinical term for images of incredibly slender women that bring on bouts of bodily self-hatred and purging as a positive impetus for starvation. One girl wrote to her pals: "I know I should be looking at Trigger Pix and making food plans for tomorrow that involve less than 400 cals."

In a peculiar outcropping of identity politics, the pro-anas have taken the name of their malady and reclaimed it as a supposedly positive identity, even as a lifestyle. In a way, the pro-anas are a perversion of a tendency for minority groups to take back derogatory terms, from the second-wave feminists calling themselves "hags" to homosexuals terming themselves "queers" to the pro-fat movement with its once-mocking names now proudly emblazoning zines such as *Fat Girl* and *Fat? So!* (The fat-acceptance movement was inaugurated by the "liberation movement," the Fat Underground in the mid 1970s; it found its institutional embodiment in the National Association to Advance Fat Acceptance, or NAAFA, which forwards a "fat politics" that seeks to remove stigma from the overweight and defends and maintains what the group considers to be their rights.)

What is most troubling about the pro-anas is that, like the teen cosmetic surgery girls and the boy bodybuilders, their identification with their disease now starts younger than ever. Ten percent of those who suffer from anorexia report the onset at ten years old or younger, and another 33 percent report the onset between ages eleven and fifteen.

But despite the horror of this illness, which leads to cessation of menstruation, premature osteoporosis, physical weakness, and even death, the pro-ana girls I communicated with did not describe their problem as "a problem." Instead, they claimed that starving was an ethos: "Nothing tastes as good as feeling thin," as one pro-ana inscribed on her site.

After their sites' removal by Yahoo, the pro-anas assumed even deeper cover and went into hiding. Linda, the pro-ana who attends a West Coast college, says that the media awareness of the pro-anas has made many of them more secretive and paranoid. "The groups are still there, the web sites, the online diaries, but now they are passworded, hidden, misleadingly named so that they can slip under the radar," says Linda. "Many people feel like we are being unfairly persecuted. After all, complications from obesity kill many more people a year than complications from anorexia."

Linda says she has "found friends who know what I am thinking and feeling and going through, and I have come to accept my driving need to be thin. . . . We are pro-thin. None of us want to die from starvation."

Pro-anas may now be off the public radar but they are still alive and unwell, creating their pastiches of fashion models and self-portraits, reassuring one another of the sanctity of wearing size 0. As long as teen girls consume images of those who consume beauty products, some minority will be willing to exchange what they need, food, for what they want, to be part of a fashion elite.

They may be the most tragically victimized of all the branded kids of Generation Y. They're certainly the most interested in showing their wounds. Like the plastic-surgery girls and the weightlifting boys, the pro-anas are symptomatic of a new sort of adolescence in which kids ratify their family's social status through looking the part. Marketers have convinced these kids that they need a specific set of physical attributes, and that their own qualities must be obviated. For the large subcultures of teens who self-brand into look-alikes with tiny waistlines, bulging biceps, deracinated noses, and copious breasts, the supposed freedom of self-creation is not a freedom at all. What they have is consumer choice, no substitute for free will.

10

Logo U

"I always thought I wouldn't be the kind of kid with an SAT tutor," says Rachel, a junior. "I never thought I would be so uptight."

Rachel sits in the central hall of the Dedham, Massachusetts, boarding school Noble & Greenough, clustered with the prep school's nonjock minority: a vegetarian, self-proclaimed socialist, a know-it-all member of the school's investment club, a snowboarder in a Hawaiian shirt who dreams of being sponsored by the snowboard company Burton. To get here, I have navigated a parking lot full of student-owned SUVs and girls carrying hockey sticks in the snow; now I find the story this klatch of kids is telling me is familiar: once-a-week SAT tutors and disappointed, befuddled parents who keep asking their kids why they aren't catapulting with ease into the Ivy League, as if it were 1972 and if they were upper-middle class and bright, all they had to do was *apply* and be admitted. "The college admissions thing has changed so much that my parents don't know what's going on—all they know is that I am not going to Harvard," says another student, Jake.

At preparatory schools such as Noble, things have changed. This is a place where the investment club has a full fifteen members who boast of picking the best penny stocks, selling when the NASDAQ was at 5,000, starting in on *The Economist* in junior high school, and "doubling their worth" back when they were freshmen. In other words it was the sort of school that used to be a feeder for the Ivies. But as Jonah Tichy, associate director of admissions at Connecticut College, says of two top New York City private schools, Collegiate and Brearley, "They used to send 80 percent of their kids to Ivies. No longer. Parents will pay $30,000 for prep schools like Milton Academy and then they believe they've paid for the right to get into the college of their choice, but they are wrong."

The increased selectivity of the colleges begets a rarified quality. That quality is intensified through the use of Early Decision programs, along with a wave of Baby Boomers' kids, with the "trophy" school. As Kate Coon, a Noble college counselor, puts it, the economically flush families whose children now do battle to attend Logo U. get into the college admissions rat race earlier than ever before. "We talk to a lot of sophomores and the parents of sophomores about colleges and test scores and extracurriculars," adds Coon. "These are fifteen-year-olds who now believe they must launch on a large campaign of self-marketing to get into their desired university, before they even know who they are. Admission to top colleges is like the American version of getting into the aristocracy."

Of course, the top-of-the-class students, as well as the legacies, have long competed to attend highfalutin, "brand name" universities. But in the last ten years, in an echo of the escalating value of designer handbags and cars, the premium put upon getting into top-ranked institutions for larger numbers of middle-class teens has become, as the teens put it, *off the hook*. A vast majority of kids who attend New York City private schools receive outside instruction in the SATs, according to the anecdotal accounts of kids and hired tutors. (The private high schools tend to support their students' single-minded quest for a brand-name identity—Harvard man or

Williams girl—as it's in their interest to do so: High admission rates at choice colleges seem to inspire alumni gifts.) These same kids routinely hire a host of others to help them out with their college admissions process, a process that has become something of an extreme sport. There are class subject tutors; tutors for achievement tests; and independent college counselors. Tutors charge anywhere from $100 an hour to $1,000 an hour; independent college counselors get from $1,000 to an amazing $29,000.

The seeds of this mania were sown years ago. While the population of teenagers has grown steadily in the last decade, the percentage of teenagers going to college has also —today 70 percent of all high school graduates attend college. Soon, there will be as many college freshmen as there were in the record year of 1981–1982, when 3 million kids graduated from high school. In 2006–2007, a projected 3 million again will graduate high school, and college enrollment is estimated to swell to 1.6 million, an increase of 16 percent from 1995. Since the late 1980s, a tool has been available to help brand colleges market themselves—the *U.S. News & World Report*'s yearly college rankings, a list that itself reflects teens' and their parents' increased desire and demand for "the best." *U.S. News* gives heavy weight to the SAT scores of a college's incoming freshmen.

Counselors and tutors all say that the *U.S. News & World Report* rankings drive the competition because, as one counselor puts it, "Selectivity is the same as quality—the harder to get into, the better it is. It all makes the SAT prep course a rite of passage of adolescence."

SOCIAL STUDIES

Sally, now a freshman at Brown University, spent the last three years of high school at her New England prep school obsessing over her SAT score, her applications, and, of course, the admissions game itself. "Kids were getting in with lots of connections and I was really worrying: I wanted to go to Harvard. If I got a B or a B-minus, my average would shift," says Sally, a small-boned blonde dressed in a white cashmere sweater, platform sneaker moon boots, and flared jeans—a casual look compared to the Katayone Adeli outfits she and her friends pick up at Barneys and wear to Upper East Side lounges.

The franticness began in Sally's sophomore year. Propelled by her parents, she says, she stayed up all night writing essays, came into New York City for SAT tutoring, and spoke on the phone twice a week to her independent college counselor. Her SAT score went from 1250 to 1450, which didn't quell her fears, she says, but simply "increased expectations. I was no longer learning, I was getting a brand put on me, getting my passport. I thought I wouldn't get a job if I didn't get into an Ivy. I felt I fell a step behind if I didn't have a counselor."

For Sally, this process was even longer than three years of high school. In another facet of kids getting older younger, many of the more privileged teenagers overwhelmed by the college admissions process had already been through the dread, the rejection, and the self-branding before—when they were toddlers. "I vividly remember being toted to the prestigious little girl's school, Episcopal," Sally says. "I remember being interviewed for preschool, and my friends also remember their interviews, like it was this watershed event. I have lived with stress for so long. In eighth grade, it was getting into high school."

For some wealthier applicants, the SAT preparation and college admission fixation now echoes a childhood of competition—lobbying for the few places available at elite primary schools in the early 1990s or, as stylish sixteen-year-old Erin in her 1970s-style dark sunglasses did, deciding she wanted to go to the University of Pennsylvania as a kid because her father went there. "I wanted to be number one. I told my parents that," says Erin. "Why did I think that going to Penn would make me number one?"

Erin and her best friend, Abigail, upper-middle-class juniors in Brooklyn, New York, mockingly dub themselves boho. The daughter of a successful film director, Erin has a very relaxed personal style. Still, she drawls that when she thinks about "the hot name colleges"—Stanford, Yale, Brown—she has panic attacks. To calm her nerves, Erin's parents send her to a weekly SAT tutor. Abigail's parents do as well, along with, as the girls tell me, "everyone else."

"Look at the mess we've gotten ourselves into, having tutors and stuff," says Abigail, swiping her sandy tendrils of hair away from her face. In their fashionably tattered T-shirts, slouched on benches with languor, both girls are ashamed that they fret over college—there's something uncool about worrying over this. The duo are suspicious of a major player in their discontent—the College Board, administrator of the SATs since 1926. "I can't believe they ask for money if you want to see your scores promptly," says Abigail, referring to a practice by which the College Board charges $20 for "rush reporting," meaning the scores are mailed out two days after they are tallied, as opposed to the normal three-week wait.

The College Board takes a lot of knocks from a lot of quarters. The nonprofit's detractors have been criticizing the board for its curiously for-profit aftertaste since at least the mid-1980s. Since that time, the company has become increasingly interested in the bottom line, recognizing the extent of the teen college-bound market and the class and social anxiety that drives parents to spend money in the name of their children's self-betterment. The board denied for years that coaching and test prep worked at all, but lately it has started to admit that test prep can boost scores; it has even started to sell its own products online, such as *One-on-One with the SAT*, a book for $29.95. The College Board has also tried to win over critics by announcing plans to launch a new SAT that contains more writing, to debut in 2005. Responding to criticisms from the SAT's biggest customer, the University of California system, which uses the exam as a primary means of selecting its students, the new and improved SAT Verbal Exam will be called the SAT Critical Reading Exam and will include a supposedly less-coachable essay test called the SAT Writing Exam.

Many remain unsatisfied. "The revisions and tweaks that the College Board are doing to the SATS aren't having educational benefit or making it less coachable," says Christina Perez, an advocate from the nonprofit group FairTest, The National Center for Fair & Open Testing, which is dedicated to K–12, university, and employment test reform. "It's not reducing the racial and economic score gaps," Perez adds. To correct these social gaps, FairTest even advocates "test score optional" college admission.

Brad MacGowan, a college counselor at a public suburban high school outside Boston, also doesn't think much of the SAT revisions. He believes the SAT still rewards "those who can afford better prep, kids whose parents have six-figure incomes," over his students who can only afford to buy a test review book or take a class at a nearby community college. (Colleges do understand the adult-dependent and costly extremes kids are going to to make it into choice colleges; Duke University asks on its application, "Whose advice did you seek for help with your essay? Was he/she helpful? What help did he/she provide?")

SCHOOL DAZE

Forty years ago, a scholastically deft teenager, especially one who was well-heeled, would stand a good chance of getting into the school he or she wanted to, joining up with the first generation of American kids who defined itself en masse by *where* they went to college.

Even fifteen years ago it was much easier to get into a brand name school than it is today. When I was sixteen, I bought a thick practice SAT test book from the Princeton Review. I knew a handful of kids who went to Princeton Review classes. As I was terrible at math, I worried that my dreadful scores would embarrass my parents, who had already poured so much money into my education. I knew they wanted me to complete our by-now shared fantasy that I would be, unlike them, *truly* middle-class. I would descend onto a sylvan campus, where everyone had whipped off a first novel and planned a congressional campaign by the age of eighteen.

In the end, I made it to mediocrity in math and attended a branded college, Brown University. The whole scenario would be far less likely today. According to the *U.S. News & World Report* in September 2001, the SAT score of Harvard admissions ranged from 1410 to 1580, at Stanford 1360 to 1560, and at Middlebury from 1350 to 1470: I scored around 1300 in 1988. (A 1300 in 1988 is different from a 1300 today—SAT scores were "recentered," raising scores up to 100 or so points.)

When I meet Adam Robinson, the elfin middle-aged whiz kid who cofounded the Princeton Review in 1982 (and sold off in 1989 and 1991), he tells me that when I was a teen fourteen years ago, there really were only three options: Do nothing, buy a book or two, or take a course with Princeton Review or Kaplan Education Centers for $500. "Now it's gone to $5,000, for private tutoring," says Robinson, who still advocates classes; he believes that peer pressure can force students to practice the exams more carefully and attentively than when they study in private. His current test preparation service, called RocketReview, specializes in preparing students who *start out* with 1300 or above and who want to aim for the highest scores. Even poorer students, he says, consider his classes a necessary investment: "Immigrant families find ways to cut corners now to afford tutors and classes—getting into a good college is what's most important. Colleges are high-risk investments: with money that exorbitant for one year of a private college, the preparation money doesn't seem so much."

These parents also know from their canny children that colleges
have put greater value on the SATs as a factor to admission. According to the National Association for College Admission Counseling
surveys, in 1989, 44 percent of college admissions officers placed
considerable importance on test scores. In 2000, 58 percent thought
test scores were key factors.

Kids attempting to brand themselves as Brown University material now are likely to spend an extraordinary amount of time and
money trying to improve their SAT scores. But they also brand
themselves to impress colleges in more onerous ways. Some kids
now choose their extracurricular activities as a means to sculpt a
more attractive profile for college admissions counselors. As college
counselor MacGowan sees it, kids now also join high school athletic
teams because of the image such team membership will project to
the colleges, says MacGowan with distaste. "They are no longer just
a way for kids to have a good time and get physically fit, but starting
very early, at the prompting of soccer moms and hockey dads, they
work to become number one on teams in their school. High school
teams are almost what college teams used to be: long practices and
team camp over the summer."

Kids' self-packaging relationships to school classes and extracurriculars are, to me, more unsettling than the strategy of taking
courses and hiring tutors to improve their test scores. A tutor men-
tions the number of kids who pretend they have performed community service, one even faking a recommendation from a priest to
verify the good works she had never performed. Many kids try to
gather letters from potentates, among them former President Bill
Clinton, in the hopes they will move jaded admissions officers.

"They obsess—if I just get my SATs to a certain point, if I help
orphans, if I get a 1760 combined score, then the path will become
clear to me, I will get into Brown and then all this would have been

worth it," says college counselor Coon, describing the self-branding that now goes into obtaining entrance to a Logo U. "They structure summers in a certain way that they wouldn't have normally, just to get in. And they are acting on information we give them—when I say I have a feeling that the college you are applying to will penalize you for not taking calculus, then they take calculus even when they don't want to."

New York City senior, Leah, eighteen, describes her private school class as rife with kids who, as she puts it, "tied themselves up in packages with bows" to get into college. They did so with unwanted, parentally obtained internships and community service here or in "Guatemala." Leah didn't do these things because she is an actress, an identity she refers to repeatedly, admitting it to be a refuge from the pressurized "clump" of kids who make perfect scores on the tests after "spending their Saturdays and Sundays at Advantage (the elite testing company) taking practice tests" and joining sports teams and advanced placement classes they have no interest in. Leah did have a private acting coach and a voice coach, though, and she saw them both at least once a week; one coach was affiliated with a university she wished to apply to (a connection that didn't pass without her notice). Leah, who has tan skin, a button nose, and presents herself as impeccably well behaved and hard working, goes to dance class and acting class and voice class during her vacations; she listens to questions carefully and answers them in full sentences; she thanks her interviewer profusely; and she even offers to pay for her Diet Coke—attributes that at first made her appear to be a woman in her twenties. Some of this maturity is one of the few happy results of her professionalization over the last few years, which was aimed at securing her admission into the college of her choice. Her program meant staying up till one in the morning on school nights studying—Leah's "package" involved heavy

SAT tutoring with three instructors to get her scores up higher than they need be, "just in case."

"It's just awful, the pressure," says Leah, plaintively, stirring her Coke. "My brother is just starting his freshman year in high school and I feel sorry for all the stress he has in store." Leah's story is far from the worst. She merely became an extreme form of herself too early, while other kids had to abandon their passions and identities and take up jerry-built ones to impress admissions officers.

Rick, sixteen, who attends a boarding school and started seeing a hired college admissions consigliere in his freshman year, puts it this way: "The name is important—you need brand recognition, if you want people to know that you are smart, and that's a serious way of letting them know that."

Rick is one of those superionized smart kids for whom even an idle conversation in the school cafeteria might turn into a heated discussion over abortion rights. When I meet him in a coffee shop, he is carrying one of the books that is part of his summer homework. (The rise of summer homework over the last few years in elite American enclaves is yet another sign of the college admissions madness, where free time is wasted not being prepped or counseled: According to the *New York Times* in 2002, summer preparation has become especially popular for "the growing numbers of students enrolled in the Advanced Placement classes" with draconian assignments for which "parents shorten vacations, leave teenagers at the library while the rest of the family is at the beach and expect all-nighters at the end of August.") But Rick, despite these top student earmarks, needs tutors and counselors as he has some flaws in his own estimation—mainly, that his semester average was a not-so-shabby 86 (only once mind you, when he was a first-semester freshman). Nevertheless, ever after, he and his family felt the GPA cast such a pall over Rick's record that he needed to start seeing an outside advisor.

"Because of my freshman first-term average mess, I thought I wasn't going to get into prep school, and then I wasn't going to get into college," Rick tells me, his speech speeding up at the horror of the thought of this downward slide.

He is more than willing to admit that he wants to go to an Ivy League school: "If you want to distinguish yourself in the private school culture, you need to get into a name school." His prep school underlines this necessity, he says, with the crests for Harvard and Yale and Amherst carved in the auditorium of his school. "You don't see Bowdoin up there," he says pointedly.

Starting his sophomore year, Rick pursued the dream of being a part of the vaunted university crests that deck his high school. He saw a college counselor, and then in the summer before his junior year he began seeing two SAT tutors in an attempt to jack his good-to-go 1400 to a spectacular 1600. Plus, there are the extracurriculars

"I'm looking into starting a business I'm doing it for myself, but I know of course that it could help on my resume," he says, choosing his words carefully and slowly, as if they were pencils he is sharpening. He purses his lips and raises the discourse from the pathos of branded educations to a more ontological plane: "I wonder sometimes—what if Yale doesn't choose to admit me and instead admits a carbon copy of me?"

Of course, the top-tier colleges have helped produce this mania by laboring to increase their value, and thus selectivity, with unprecedented vigor in the last decade. When they churn out logo-ed merchandising and "distance learning" programs, they reap money internationally from their good names. They also market far more heavily than in the past, setting their sights on better *U.S. News & World Report* rankings, sending out a media blitz of glossy brochures and come-ons, an extension of the flogging of teen-oriented products that has taken hold of Generation Y. There are admissions conferences at which the marketing and packaging of a school are of the utmost importance, and they are often attended by deans of enrollment management. These deans receive pressure from all quarters and for many reasons, including business reasons: One of the components of Moody's Investment Service's bond rating for a college is the SAT scores of incoming freshmen.

One the most spectacular examples of new cutthroat extremes the college admissions business has reached happened in July 2002, when Princeton University's admissions office tapped into the Yale University admissions Web site to check on Yale applicants. (These applicants included that of President Bush's niece, Lauren Bush.) A more common symptom of these extremes, though, is the ever-rising rates of early decision (ED) and early action applicants, part of the culture begotten by the *U.S. News* branding of university life.

Under early action, student applicants are given advance notice of their acceptance to a college, but need not agree to attend; the offer stays open. Under early decision, students are required to accept an institution's offer, or the offer will be withdrawn. More than four hundred colleges and universities around the country offer these programs, one of their main purposes being to improve school rankings: Once a kid has been extended an early-decision or early-action acceptance, his or her test scores enter the data bank. And what kind of kids seek early action and, especially, early decision? The savviest—the students who attend exclusive schools and who are also often the most highly tutored. What sort of kids don't? Less privileged kids, those who are either not in the loop because they attended public schools or kids whose decisions about schools have to take into account the availability of financial aid. Few in the college business profess to liking early decision: Most admit that it has become a norm because it burnishes the reputations of big-business universities and thus creates monetary gain for them. As

James Fallows has written, most critically, in the *Atlantic Monthly* in September 2001, ED adds to the "insane intensity" of "parents' obsession about getting their children into one of a handful of prestigious colleges" while benefiting test prep companies such as Kaplan Education Centers. Kaplan's vice president, Seppy Basili, remarked that because of the prevalence of ED, "kids come to us earlier, prepare earlier, prepare more and from a business aspect that's great." Early decision has also come under so much fire recently that Richard C. Levin, president of Yale University, suggested its abolition.

Joyce Slayton Mitchell, director of college advising at the elite Nightingale-Bamford School in New York City and author of *Winning the Heart of the College Admissions Dean: An Expert's Advice for Getting Into College*, finds early action's ascendance troubling. "Kids do insist on the designer names—I gotta go to Yale, they say. Meanwhile every year it's more competitive for privileged kids," says Mitchell. Privileged is right: I had seen the rows and rows of Nightingale girls in their gray uniforms, shiny hair, and terrifically short skirts, each girl wearing accessories that give her individuality—clunky shoes here, a sparkly pin there—but I try to feel their pain in spite of their evident wealth and immaculate breeding. "Kids are so programmed to time crunch that they spend three hours a night doing homework, which now has hours of tutoring on top," says Mitchell. "This is not where their hearts want to be. This isn't what they should do in the summer."

Mitchell is a strong critic of early decision, which she believes adds to the dehumanizing pressure. "I've been thinking about why I find early decision so objectionable," she has written, in a typed statement to her students' parents; she goes on to enumerate the reasons for her antipathy, among them that early decision cuts decision time in half for teenagers. "Early decision is really just an advantage to the colleges," Mitchell tells me before shooing me out of her office to greet the first of a line of skittish girls with sleek long hair, all waiting, nervously, for her to look at their applications.

The Gold-Plated Tutors

Especially when applying for early decision and early action, wealthier teenagers now feel the need to self-brand, to develop college essays and interview stories replete with talking points that sell their attributes to the name college of their choice. It can start with SAT prep at fourteen and college counseling at fifteen. If they buy into the logic of the Johns Hopkins Talent Search, they may well take the SAT at fourteen to enroll in summer courses, and they must achieve 430 in math and 430 in verbal to qualify for consideration in the "talent search." The Johns Hopkins Talent Search literature claims that the process introduces "an important test, the SAT, to young students in a 'low stakes' environment."

Rather than becoming themselves, they now pour all their young energy into constructing their teen brands ("the altruist," "the athlete") so they will appeal to another long-branded entity, the Ivy League college. They prepare "Who Am I?" statements—I am loyal, I am generous, I have overcome diabetes, I am a feminist. The independent counselor may use technological and rather refined methods, among them video, when asking them hundreds of questions in a mock interview so that the kid can see, in the words of one counselor, "how they interview, their body language." College Coach, a Boston-area coaching service that entices clients with the promise of "established marketing tools to emphasize your strengths," makes obvious the commercial quality of the skills it teaches high school students.

In New York City, a hotbed of college-as-brand culture, parents and their children hire not just anyone but try to see the "best" tutors or college counselors. One of these top counselors is Alexandra Self. "'My kid has to get into Harvard or Princeton or I will kill myself,'" she quotes me, her voice rising in an imitation of her client parents' hysteria. "The kids are getting into name schools for their parents, conferring status upon their parents—it's been like this for seven years."

I sit with Ms. Self, as she is known to her students, in her home office, on Manhattan's Upper East Side. There's a distinct air of the godmother to Self: She is superpoised, her visage resembling that of Mary Tyler Moore.

But what the thirty-five kids Self works with each year find most comforting about her is not her pleasant looks or the landscape paintings, the oak desks, and the brocade pillows dotting the apartment. It's her ability to package them—to make high school students into saleable entities through their essays and carefully curated extracurricular activities and on-point, rehearsed interviews. "The fear factor is immense," says Self. "They are interested in their family's ability to make the right connections. Packaging students [to get them into college] is the name of the game."

And as wealthy teens have come to see their futures as just another designer product, they may treat their tutors as if they were designer goods as well. One New York City tutor remarks that a wealthy pupil thought of him as an accessory, "like a Kate Spade bag." Plenty of other tutors feel they're treated as the hired help. The private SAT tutoring racket, like so many aspects of teen life, gives Generation Y the message that they can buy their way into a permanent upper-middle class or even into the upper class. (And often, as in any other focus of adolescent consumerism, peer pressure is at work. A recent graduate of the elite Manhattan private school

Dalton told me that she hired a tutor only because everyone else she knew had one.)

"The parents have their yoga, Valium, and then they call us," says Nile Lanning, a well-regarded New York City SAT tutor. Lanning charges $375 for ninety minutes of tutoring, which is far from the high end of the tutoring business; she jokes that she is considered a bargain, and in a business where tutors charge as much as $500 an hour and anxiety is at an all time high, she could charge more and get away with it.

Lanning underlines the tutor-as-designer-object element of this process when she notes with dismay that "looking right" for the role is very important—"dressing well, being young and attractive." She's a slender blonde of thirty-four. She is also an acerbic and clever Oxford University graduate, qualities evident in her own informal history of the SAT private tutoring explosion published in *New York* magazine in 2000. Having a tutor in the 1980s, she wrote, was a kind of "social suicide" for kids and for their parents; it was an embarrassing "acknowledgment of intellectual inadequacy, faulty parenting, and general mediocrity." But now that the private schools and the eminent public ones have shifted radically, students are deeply, constantly aware of the effect their grades and SAT scores have on their futures. And so tutors became first acceptable and then desirable.

Within the tutoring and counseling market, there are now brands of tutor that parents and kids rightly or wrongly buy into. One of these brands in New York City is Advantage Testing. The costliest Advantage tutor charges $565 an hour, high prices that are disparaged by another eminent SAT counselor as "feeding on parents' despair—kids need ten hours of help and it can be in a course setting, and that's about all you can do." One describes these methods as akin to a séance. (Advantage also taps into the brand consciousness of New York teenagers in the know—the wealthiest girls I spoke with all saw tutors from the company. One Uptown girl was quoted in *W.* magazine as comparing Advantage to a Prada bag.) There's also the travel angle—kids can take a two-week Stanford course for $5,400 while vacationing, and tutors accompany the families on vacation for $1,400 a day. The most popular services remain the Princeton Review courses, whose enrollment has risen tenfold, and Kaplan Education Centers, whose numbers have risen twentyfold. Even these meat-and-potatoes classes, which both guarantee that students' scores will rise 100 points above those achieved on their first diagnostic exams, don't come cheap. Princeton costs between $800 and $900, and Kaplan $859.

The business is competitive and stakes are high, so it comes as no surprise that there are internecine snipes about the "real" value of certain college counselors. The more audacious the pricing, the more enthusiastic the sniping, so I heard plenty about Kat Cohen, founder of a college counseling outfit called IvyWise. Cohen sells a platinum package: $28,995 for twenty-four sessions and an hour of phone time each week, usually dispersed across junior and senior years. Cohen says she works with forty of the most selective colleges and takes "a holistic approach" with her charges; by "holistic" she means getting kids to fill in the gaps, perhaps with an athletic regime, a psychologist, an academic tutor, better test scores, internships, application review, hand holding, interview preparation, and generally improving "their brag sheet of extra curricula activities, hobbies, and work experience."

"They are coming to me younger and younger—seventh, eighth, ninth grade—so they can get in early and reserve a place," says Cohen. "They have to start taking SAT IIs in ninth grade, and enrolling in summer programs." As for the kids' increased brand consciousness about college admissions: "If you hear about Bayer

Aspirin all your life, you need that brand and only buy that brand. College names are like that for these kids."

But more often than not, Cohen and independent coaches like her are also trading on the celebrity aura of the brand college to get kids and their parents to pony up the cash for their services. One college coaching service hawks itself by promising that if a child sticks with them, the child will never be embarrassed by the college sticker on his or her car window.

ALL IN THE FAMILY

Parents have no small role in the building of Logo U., a way of thinking about and applying to college that thrives in the New York City area, in Boston, around Washington, D.C., in Chicago, and, to a lesser extent, in Los Angeles. Although the parents may well have attended obscure universities, that fact doesn't always keep them from pelting the newly hired college counselors with demands that their kids make it into a trinity of the top schools: Harvard, Yale, and Princeton (in fact, it probably compels them to do so). In a new development, many middle-class parents now figure it's all or nothing: If their kids aren't accepted by an Ivy League school, they will have to settle for a public university or a local college. "Second" or "third" private schools cost the same $40,000 as Harvard; these parents don't see the percentage value in paying that much for an off-brand. It's a story that Connecticut College's admissions officer, Jonah Tichy, repeats, saying that parents may well refuse to spend $35,000 a year on an institution that they have never heard of. "Even if the parents are themselves deep into six figures, they want familiarity, they want other people to have heard of colleges their children attend," he says. "I see parents leading their child's admissions process and their sons following sheepishly along."

The tutors and counselors tell cloak-and-dagger tales of kids learning to be strategic, and at times deceptive, about their increased dependence on those in their profession. Sometimes the kids keep their less-cherished classmates in the dark and tell only their popular peers, as a social favor, about a beloved tutor or independent college counselor. Parents embarrassed by tutoring devise ways to prevent its detection; for example, one mother doesn't want her children seen working with a tutor at Starbucks; another asks that her daughter be let out the back door of a tutor's home office rather than the front entrance to avoid detection by her fellow teens. The kids may well follow suit, mimicking their parents' shame. Tutors say they often serve as a buffer by protecting kids from hectoring parents and the unfair expectations these parents have of their children's admissions potential. Tutors also persuade unenlightened, embarrassed parents to accept untimed tests for children who have learning disabilities, and they dissuade parents who wish to write their children's college essays out of an unchecked desire for their kids to succeed.

"Parents tell me their degrees from colleges like Denison have held them back," says Self. "They see getting their kids into name-brand schools as getting the credentials they did not have." This desperation can sometimes lead parents to encourage dishonesty in their children. Another high-end tutor recounts one Wall Street father who was so determined to inflate his son's SAT score that he found a test site where, he told his son, it was reputed that one could cheat.

"The process is very hard on the parents," says the mother of two girls, one a recent New York private school graduate who is now a college sophomore, the other a private high school senior. "My friends and I are bemoaning the whole situation with the tutor and the coach that cost a bloody fortune and there's no way out of it—if you are in Manhattan everyone does it, my child is begging me to go to the tutor. I was shocked that my child would attend a New York private school and wouldn't go to a well-known school—then what I call 'the new reality' of admissions set in,'" this mother says, a trace of bitterness evident.

The same mother confesses that she is "much more ambitious about my daughters than I was about myself." Now she sees the drawbacks of that drive. She followed the name recognition fad and it did not lead to happiness; she encouraged her older daughter to attend the "best school she got into, not the best school for her," and now finds her child full of malaise.

There are alternatives to the *U.S. News & World Report* view of colleges and academic success, however. The National Survey of Student Engagement (NSSE) asks students about the quality of their academic life and derives its rankings from their replies. Perhaps tellingly, few of the prestige name colleges—367 of the 1,400 four-year institutions in the United States—had signed up to participate in the NSSE survey of spring 2002.

Ken Danford, founder, director, and educator at NorthStar, a center for unschooled teens (unschooled teens are kids who choose to educate themselves rather than attend conventional schools or be taught by their parents) derides the whole SAT testing process as the crux of the problem of conventional schooling. "We raise the stakes for insignificant things like our eighth-grade transcripts. Does anyone care, when you are on your book tour, what you got on your SAT?" asks Danford (I joke that for me, as a writer of a book about adolescence, they may very well care; still, he has a point). For Christina Perez of FairTest, the role social class plays in the branded college economy is a symptom of a corroded system.

Still, back in the world of Logo U., teens continue to fax their essays to the college counselors, who tear them apart and glue them back together in a slick package ready for the colleges. "I don't think coaching is fair," remarks one affluent girl, who was tutored weekly by Advantage. "But I felt I had to get into a good college and be successful. I did get in and I am glad. It's a double-edged sword."

11

Almost Famous:
The Teen Literary Sensations

Toward the end of the 1990s, a new strain of teen self-branding took hold, the teen memoir and its companion, the teen-written novel. For the most part, one can judge these books by their covers. There's *Katie.com: My Story,* which bears the image of a lost-looking little girl inviting the reader into the then seventeen-year-old author Katie Tarbox's realm of underage sexual victimization. There's *Crazy,* Benjamin Lebert's account of his deflowering and alienation, which shows a cover photo of Lebert at sixteen, pretty, bruised, and big-lipped, like a still from a Larry Clark movie. There's Rebbecca Ray's *Pure*—fourteen-year-old loses virginity to thirty-one-year-old man—which beckons with a composition: miniskirt, birch-tree-thin pubescent legs, and Adidas trainers, all framed by a field of daisies.

The writers are as effectively packaged as their books, and that shouldn't be surprising. For today's youth, as for so many social groups before them, the ability to be heard arises from their acumen at selling themselves. They do this by mimicking "adult" formats and covering adult themes of personal trauma to create first-hand accounts that satisfy adult interest and prurience. Raised in the era of confessional literature, having seen how secrets can be traded for celebrity, teenagers are selling their own experiences before they know they have a story that should be protected as their own or a self that has yet cohered. They also believe, being the children of the Oprah and Clinton age, that public confessions of sin and remorse, a recounting of their histories of abuse, will help expiate wrongdoing or pain.

This notion of healing-through-telling emerges from an unholy hodgepodge of influences: Saint Augustine, Jean-Jacques Rousseau, Catholicism, Romantic poetry, Southern Baptism, and Anne Sexton. But the teen self-branding writers don't tend to define themselves as part of a history, as having been encouraged by a culture of confession as well as by the popularity of a newly minted genre, the fiction-memoir.

One fiction-memoirist is Ned Vizzini, now twenty-one. He was fifteen when the *New York Press,* a weekly newspaper known for its expressive first-person vignettes and its libertarian, sensationalist politics, began publishing the autobiographical essays about the prom and girlfriends and music that compose his debut book, *Teen Angst? Naaah. . . .* When he was eighteen, Free Spirit Publishing bought the essays to publish as a collected volume; in 2002, it was optioned by Jane Startz Productions for a film to be backed by a first-look deal at Miramax. The book is now being reprinted as a trade paperback by Random House.

"I wanted my book to be easy to follow, like television," Ned tells me when we meet. He has thick eyebrows, dark eyes, and bristly brown short hair; he is fashionably late, but not particularly sorry. He peels off his headphones and plonks down at a table and immediately grabs the *New York Post,* abandoned by the last vente latte drinker. He starts reading it out loud—the tone is half senior-class clown, half talk show host. "Mayor Michael Bloomberg celebrates

Groundhog Day! The *Post*'s latest young beauty! Look, they say she's gorgeous? Does she look gorgeous to you? I don't think so."

Enough fun. He takes his book out of his bag.

"I wanted my book to be more gripping than television actually, so I did it all in very short chapters with sidebars," he says, thumbing through the brightly bound volume.

What makes Vizzini a self-brander is not his likeable palaver or his charming book. It is his automatic and precocious grasp of the marketing of his work. I encounter him in a month that he spends awaiting news of what will be done with his teen memoir—television show or movie?—but Vizzini doesn't lounge in career limbo. He is busy maintaining an efficient Web site, Nedvizzini.com. He answers every e-mail, he says. As he puts it, he makes the rounds, and because of his efforts, he's sold 15,000 copies so far of a book published by a relatively small independent press.

"I have hand-sold it to booksellers," says Vizzini. "I speak at schools and associations. I hustle to get blurbs—blurbs are important. I did interviews. I sent it to young influential people: I had to target it, you know? I sent it to Spielberg's kids; I hear they read it. I talked to *Talk* magazine about it (now defunct) with the same fervor as I talked to Dorothy Whatsit in Vancouver. Look, people read small presses. My book publisher calls it viral marketing: A teenager in Vancouver reads it and tells their friend."

Vizzini is as thoughtful about his authorial financial arrangements as he is about forwarding his writerly fame. "I was eighteen when I signed my contract. I should have sent it to a lawyer because I gave away my media rights. Now I don't get extra profits," he says. But then I am reminded of his age and his appealing guilelessness: He offers me a sip of his caramel apple cider and wants to show how his book's illustrator made his prom date's breasts bigger than they were.

Like the other teen writers and memoirists, Vizzini has internalized the promotional ethos of the age he grew up in. It is hard to view him as a pawn in anyone else's scheme; but it is just as hard to see an iota of resistance to the corporate, celebrity-made swirl that has seized the imaginations of adolescents in the last decade.

PRODIGY OR PRODUCT?

It's been over fifty years since Holden Caulfield ran away from boarding school, forty-seven since Lolita drove Humbert Humbert mad with lust, and roughly thirty since Judy Blume and her lubricious teen menagerie ushered in the first golden age of young adult fiction, the so-called problem novels. In short, young adult literature written by adults is very young, barely a hundred years old. Of course, there were the classic adult texts that were also consumed by teenage readers in the previous epochs—Daniel Defoe's *Robinson Crusoe* and Jonathan Swift's *Gulliver's Travels*, James Fenimore Cooper's frontier stories and Washington Irving's ghost tales. But substantial works directly aimed at adolescents emerged only at the beginning of the twentieth century, with the *Anne of Green Gables* series and *The Secret Garden,* and it wasn't until after World War II that the fashion for psychological testing and research of adolescents lent itself to the founding of an age-appropriate literature: young adult literature, or YA. The genre really took hold in the 1960s, when the swoony romances and astringent, character-building tales of the early postwar period—sunshine-filled high schools, nuclear families—gave way to the socially concerned problem novels. The problem novels dealt with divorce, pregnancy, and inner-city life.

Today, the genre is on an upswing. And with more books being published for older teenagers, more slots are available for young writers to also start publishing. That includes teen best-sellers such as *Smack,* the story of a teen junkie; *Speak,* the story of a teen who goes nearly mute after a rape; and *Holes,* the story of a teen sentenced to hard labor at a reform school. It also includes books that emulate the voices of the most privileged, brand-obsessed girls on the Upper East Side of Manhattan, a veritable junior *Sex and the City. Gossip Girl,* published by Little, Brown children's books and written by thirty-one-year-old Cecily von Ziegesar is one such example. It includes a host of Upper East Side private schools, Pucci dresses, and MTV2. Our protagonist's mind is "a mental Palm Pilot." In a chapter titled "An Hour of Sex Burns 360 Calories," the protagonist, Blair, accompanies her mother to a party; her mother wears "the fitted, graphite-beaded cashmere dress that Blair had helped her pick out from Armani, and little black velvet mules. A year ago she wouldn't have fit into the dress, but she had lost twenty pounds since she met Cyrus. She looked fantastic. Everyone thought so." The book's sleek promotional Web site encourages girls to share their "dish"—the stories of their BFs (boyfriends, in *Gossip Girl* parlance). Like the film *Cruel Intentions, Gossip Girl* depicts a teenaged label-obsessed urban overclass. Young adult novels about Manhattan kids are now far more worldly than they were in the past, when the genteel tales of preteens trapped overnight in the Metropolitan Museum or of a girl brainiac finding refuge from twittish classmates by spending hours scribbling in her diary were the high point of youth social adventurousness.

The popularity and proliferation of young adult fiction coincided with the emergence of "youth culture" in the 1960s. It was also in the late 1960s and early 1970s that the "youth opinion" was first solicited publicly, so much so that Joyce Maynard could write "An 18-Year-Old Looks Back on Life" for the Sunday magazine of the *New York Times,* and YA problem novelist Susan Eloise Hinton could start publishing her series of rough-and-tumble Western novels when she was seventeen (she began writing them at fifteen).

"And I—I am 18, caught in the middle. Mine is the generation of unfulfilled expectations," wrote Maynard, presaging a period thirty years hence when young writers routinely would look "back on life." Maynard goes on, "'When you're older,' my mother promised, 'you can wear lipstick.' But when the time came, of course, lipstick wasn't being worn. . . . 'Just wait till we can vote,' I said, bursting with 10-year-old fervor, ready to fast, freeze, march and die for peace and freedom as Joan Baez, barefoot, sang 'We Shall Overcome.' Well, now we can vote, and we're old enough to attend rallies and knock on doors and wave placards, and suddenly it doesn't seem to matter any more."

Meanwhile, Hinton published the *The Outsiders*, a first-person tale about gang life and teen murder, in 1967. Soon critics called her the voice of youth. By the 1980s, she could also be termed the scriptwriter of youth (although she didn't write scripts herself); four of her books had been adapted as films, three starring the then teen heartthrob Matt Dillon.

Hinton was followed by Cameron Crowe, author of the book that became the 1981 film *Fast Times at Ridgemont High*, for which he went "undercover" as a just post-teen in a high school and wrote about the experience. Crowe also wrote articles for *Rolling Stone* that formed the hub of his 2000 film *Almost Famous*, about his experience on the road with a famous rock band, the story told from the perspective of a teenage fan and journalist. Neither Crowe nor Hinton, however, wrote about other people; their books were never (explicitly) about themselves. Personality-driven youth writing was yet to come.

As for teen writers of the 1980s, I recall, as a published kid writer who drew on my limited life experience for my poetry, that there were few teen writers whose work saw publisher's galleys. Perhaps that's why the teen writers I knew were, in contrast to today's savvy and congenial authors, rather ethereal, aspiring with all the necessary grandiosity to be any romantic figure who wrote young and died pure. These young writers were inspired by sources quite different from the current teen memoirists' pop pantheon, best-selling authors such as Kathryn Harrison, Michael Crichton, and Candace Bushnell. For us, branding oneself and achieving some kind of celebrity from one's young adventures were simply not part of the scenario.

ADULT ADULATORS

One of the ways self-branding teenagers ascend is with the help of an adult. Teen writers tell me of their admiration for Amelia Atwater-Rhodes, an eighteen-year-old author who has just published her fourth novel—she swiftly produces sequels while still young so that she can "leverage" her brand. When she was thirteen, Atwater-Rhodes "worked" with an English teacher on selling her first manuscript, a teacher who happened to be a literary agent: it was published on her fourteenth birthday.

Adults tend to be keys to the teen writers' success. These grownups may be friends of the kids' parents, especially if the teen writer is eighteen-year-old Nick McDonnell, the author of *Twelve;* his godfather, Hunter S. Thompson, and the novelist Richard Price have already sung the praises of *Twelve* (McDonnell just happens to be the son of his mentors' powerful pal Terry McDonnell, the managing editor of *Sports Illustrated*.)

For less well-connected teen writers, befriending famous adults who will protect them and aid and abet their careers is the way to go. JT Leroy contacted novelists Mary Gaitskill and Dennis

Cooper, and also songwriter Suzanne Vega, who embraced the charismatic Leroy when he was in his mid-teens. Cooper edited Leroy's first novel, and Gaitskill, Cooper, and Jerry Stahl read it at venues around the country. Adult fetish photographer Eric Kroll discovered the now twenty-two-year-old photographer Natacha Merritt on the Web and smoothed the way for publication of her book *Digital Diaries*, a collection of photographic self-portraits documenting her sex life from teenager to young adult.

HARRIET THE SPY CAM

As it has with most things teen, the Web has been a factor in the new teen memoirs. Tarbox, for instance, wrote *Katie.com: My Story* after suffering a Web-related sexual trauma: Her narrative expertly brings the reader into a tale of teen violation by a pedophile. Her book documents her pain. When she was thirteen, she met Frank Kufrovich online, believing that he was a twenty-three-year-old named Mark. They arranged to meet after months of courtship, but her online crush turned out to be a forty-one-year-old who molested her. Afterwards, shamed and ostracized in her hometown of New Canaan, Connecticut, she switched to St. Paul's boarding school in New Hampshire, where she ultimately turned her miserable Web episode into a memoir. In truth, Katie was never comfortable with the New Canaan boys who, she writes in *Katie.com*, examined "girls under a microscope," and her book can be read as an exchange of one sort of scrutiny and awareness for another. It is as if Katie were trying to vault over the ever-more intense minicelebrity systems in her town and high school, with their high premium on designer clothes and beauty, first through her awful Internet encounter and then through her ascendance to actual national celebrity as a popular author with a tawdry past.

"New Canaan was a town filled with beautiful people," Tarbox writes, "and I was pretty much the opposite." Meanwhile, America Online (AOL), the Web, and chat rooms were "an entire new world" that was "limitless." Online she was unhindered by her appearance or adolescent physical awkwardness. In New Canaan, she says, she would never wear sweatpants into town for fear of ridicule from her affluent, branded peers. Online, she could "take down walls." The Web gives Katie Tarbox's teen memoir trajectory—the escape from the real branded universe to a virtual one, and then finally to a branded authorial identity—a new twist .

I visit Katie at her family's two-story Connecticut house in the spring of 2000. We talk in her room, where a Gateway computer and a Sony Vaio and her whole life of technological unhappiness vies with the self-contained good-girlism of her Laura Ashley bedspread set and wicker furnishings; later, we sit in her family's dark sitting room, a room decorated with gold lamps and some chinoiserie. This is the house of her stepfather and her mother, who, she writes in her book, "lived at the office." While not quite a tell-all, her book certainly tells a lot.

Tarbox writes in *Katie.com*, "Suddenly I realized that this was a grown man who was giving me my first real kiss, not a fuzzy-faced teenager, not someone my own age. Something inside me snapped. Now I didn't want this at all. But I couldn't speak. I hesitantly pulled away. He lifted my shirt and grabbed my breast."

Tarbox says that she wrote *Katie.com* for "therapeutic" purposes and also because she "thought it might help other victims of pedophiles to stop blaming themselves." It is also clear that *Katie.com* helped her redefine herself within her community—from lonely outcast to marginalized sexual molestation survivor to celebrity writer. It's a familiar alchemy, one that many adults seek when they attempt to become famous or even simply successful professionals after being bullied or hurt as children. The acceleration of the process is new, however. Before now, kids didn't seek refuge from their peers through a fame gained by their suffering.

While capable of ambivalence and even refusal about the ordinary ways in which middle-class teen life is commodity-driven, Tarbox doesn't double guess self-marketing. Like the other new teen writers, Tarbox spent many hours in her senior year checking her book's ranking on Amazon and building a Web site, KatieT.com, to promote her book. Tarbox became a morning talk-show favorite for her self-possession—she tends to talk of her generation in the third-person.

The noncelebrity writer kids responding to Tarbox's book also use the Web as a platform for their own confessions. On Amazon.com, one writes that she, too, has fallen for someone online. "This book was scary to me because the beginning seemed like it could come from my life," wrote a Katie fan. "I am a thirteen-year-old, and I live in a small (snobbish) town in Connecticut (quite near Katie's home town of New Caanan). I also went through a very similar experience on the net, though not up to the point of meeting the person. I started reading this book at ten o'clock, and finished it off later that night around two A.M."

Marty Beckerman, nineteen, is a less successful self-branding teen sex memoirist who has also uses the Web and martybeckerman.com to get his book *Death to All Cheerleaders: One Adolescent Journalist's Cheerful Diatribe Against Teenage Plasticity* out there as well as his upcoming *Generation Slut: A Brutal Feel-Up Session with Todays's Sex-Crazed Adolescent Populace*. The former, as a selection of vitriolic, lustful essays that he published when he was seventeen with Infected Press, a publisher he created. His site lists the publications that have printed his work; they range from the homey-sounding local paper, the *Anchorage Daily News Review,* to the not-so-homey-sounding *Penthouse Online*. Indeed, Beckerman's writing is lascivious enough to be at home in the latter: "Goddamn, something about the possibility of getting caught just sends a warm shiver down my testicles," Beckerman writes. "Not yet, Penis. But soon. Very, very soon. The door creaks open; the house is dark and the girl's parents are fast asleep. My heart is pounding and the adrenaline is coursing through my veins like black tar heroin." Beckerman writes contemptuously that his generation should receive the appellation "Generation Slut" because of his peers' rates of sexual activity. He then proves his own membership in said generation by hiring a prostitute as a prom date.

The professionalized teen writers who use the Web for their content or to help them in their self promotion are a small slice of the Internet-based teen confessional zeitgeist. On the Web, there's a potpourri of amateur teen diaries, a backdrop to the published teen works. These teen diarists take the public stage on the Internet as they jockey for an audience and remuneration. The money can be significant: A girl named Ashley Power has gathered such a following with her Web site, Goosehead, that she now has a market for T-shirts and sweatshirts bearing her own logo. Power has even started her own teen Web soap, *Whatever.* Part of the brand is the bona fide teen-ness of Ashley's Web voice: "My life is pretty much like every other teenager," she writes on her Web site. "I have my own Web site like a lot of you do. I like hanging out with my buds, the phone is always attached to my ear, which makes my Dad crazy."

The most unabashed of the teen diarists who suffer and seduce in public are the Web cam girls. These girls are essentially in competition for viewers, and they make money by attracting users. The Web cam girls pose for the cams: They comb their hair and hang out, sometimes half-undressed. On their sites, such voguing is bordered by their diary entries and message boards.

Lana, eighteen when I spoke to her, is one such popular Web cam girl. She exhorts users to stalk her and love her. As an incentive, she wears tight T-shirts and recounts her life history to anyone who will read it, all with self-effacing good humor: "My parents had sex back on march 7th, 1982 and 9 short months later i hatched from my little egg . . . i was just a quiet little gal. fast forward a decade and a half and i am the same exact person . . . just with bigger boobs."

The Web cam diaries feature wish lists, an enumeration of the Web girls' taste in electronic gifts, such as digital cameras and video games. Their hope is that adult fans will send them something from the list. One asks for video games, CDs, and Sailor Moon dolls. Lana admits the presents are part of the bottom line of having a site, the reason she unveils herself in writing and pictures to countless strangers. "The cuter you are, the more presents you get off your wish lists," Lana explains. Her gifts from "creepy guys" have so far included a digital camera. "Who is going to turn a digital camera down?" she asks, dreamily.

Lana tells me she started playing around with Web cams when she was fourteen but became an official Web cam girl only two years ago, in 2000. "I found this Web cam community of teenagers," she recalls, adding that "the pretty Web cam girls are all friends with each other. I liked the attention. People return everyday to watch my Web cam diary and read my writing." Although she also shows off her figure, she singles out the Web cam girl Nay, short for Renee—as part of the crowd of teen Web girls who "show skin in an attempt to get more viewers, and put up nude pics," Lana says. "A lot of them are young and they are trying to get lots of hits. Everyone wants to be popular and famous." (Lana herself has become relatively famous from her site and has even appeared on a television talk show be-cause of her Web renown.)

All the teen writers—published memoirists and fiction writers, Web diarists, and Web cam exhibitionists alike—have understood that teen bodies are products. It makes sense to these teens to merchandise their bodies and experiences. Teen authors have become the architects of their own trademarked identities, strong-willed and mercenary in equal measure.

TRUTH AND BEAUTY

Of course, some of the new teen writing is actually impressive.

"The johns don't talk, don't hardly look at me," JT Leroy writes in his first novel, *Sarah*. "They handle me rough, like a steering wheel they have to bully through a tight turn. They blame me if they're too drunk and they blame me if they ain't drunk enough. . . . Also cost me a good number of black eyes and a few chips on my teeth."

In one scene, a pedophilic john realizes that the hero, whose "beautiful little baby nipples" cause him such delight, is actually a boy and not a preteen girl: "Lymon pushes me back down, which so surprises me I stay down. I feel him spreading my legs with his hands. His fingers probe between my legs . . . 'Oh, sweet Jesus!' he says louder . . . 'What are you?!' he screams. 'Are you the devil?!'" In my favorite paragraph, Leroy writes: "I loved watching her [his mother] lick her finger and run it gently under my eyes. It always reminded me of those nature films of a mother bird regurgitating food into its baby's mouth."

Leroy is the most compelling of the teen writers because he hustled his writing career more fiercely than any of them. At the same time, he is one of the most serious youth writers out there. Leroy has branded himself wildly, through a personal Web site, which at one point sold one of *Sarah's* artifacts, a raccoon's penis, as a totem. At the same time, Leroy half refuses the branding phenomena, which in the tradition of reclusive writers and rock stars worldwide is a marketing gambit all of its own.

Leroy's success rests not on his vital, associative writing but on the personal hook—his real-life history of young suffering and his underage street-hustler chic. Growing up in Appalachia, he was, like the boy in *Sarah,* trained by his prostitute mother to be a cross-dressing truck-stop teen hustler. He says he saved his soul and perhaps his life when, as a West Coast street kid, he began writing. In short order, he acquired a column at the *New York Press.* When he was thirteen, he began *Sarah.* He says that at first, he was disgusted by the way the book industry "sensationalized" his age and his background. When he was offered a book deal that same year, he just froze. He stopped writing for two years.

Leroy has since learned to stop worrying and appreciate marketing. At one point, *Sarah* reached Number 10 on the *Los Angeles Times* best-seller list. Then director Gus Van Sant bought the movie rights (it's now in the early stages of production) and became a friend. A Manhattan art gallery put up a show of photos of Leroy cross-dressing. There's the television screenplay he wrote, which is destined to be a program produced by Diane Keaton and Gus Van Sant for HBO. Rock star Shirley Manson of the band Garbage writes songs about him and is competing with Angelina Jolie for the role of his mother in the film version of his novel. Rock star Courtney Love e-mails him.

Pitching himself as an icon in limited supply, Leroy has also taken his cultivated, fragile persona, with its Garbo-like allure, on the road—and demand has increased accordingly. For instance, the only photo of him in circulation, the self-portrait on the back of *Sarah,* shows an androgynous boy with curly blonde tendrils (the photo is also the cover of Dennis Cooper's book *Period,* where Leroy is the prototype for a teen character who is hacked to death.)

He is a brilliant example of self-creation. When I talk to him by phone (he refuses to meet in person), he greets me in a whisper. I hear a baby crying in the background, and a man's voice as well. I become unsure. I'm not sure this person I'm talking to is JT Leroy, or that JT Leroy is in fact male, or that JT Leroy wrote his own work. All these mysteries add up to a highly marketable mystique.

As much as he appears to confess all in his writing, including the most dreadful sexual and physical victimization and poverty, and the most intense depression and neglect, Leroy actually holds the most basic details of his ordinary life away from his readers, his interviewers, and even his mentors. This seems as much the result of canny self-marketing as it is of genius or neurosis: When he recounts his bruised and bewildered coming of age, he tends to segue easily into talk of his movie deal. He is also a self-mythologist: he claims, for example, to have started the (untrue) rumor that Dennis Cooper actually wrote *Sarah.* Many of his fans admit they haven't met him in person for any sizable amount of time and that they, too, have wondered whether he is a hoax. Around the time of the publication of *The Heart Is Deceitful Above All Things,* a short-story collection he wrote as a teenager, Leroy played up that mystique. He was featured in *Vanity Fair,* and in what could be taken as a parody of his own persona, he was photographed clad in a tutu and an owl-feather mask. His celebrity was telegraphed as much by what you couldn't see as by what you could. It was a successful approach— everything about Leroy is singular and gauzy.

At times Leroy and a handful of others seem to transcend their self-marketing. But it remains true that Leroy's authenticity and talent are inextricably coupled with cultivation of celebrity.

"I'm way into pimping *Sarah,*" he says.

I WAS A TEENAGE WRITER

Most book publishers look at new books to see how they might resemble works already in existence. They think of writers as resembling other writers. When it comes to teen authors, publishers often
have the authors of New York nightlife fiction of the 1980s in mind.
But there's a crucial and telling difference: Those decadent young
novelists of the 1980s were usually in their late twenties when they
debuted. The kids who are thought of as their descendents haven't
yet attended college.

In the *New Yorker* in 2002, eighteen-year-old Nick McDonnell
was vaunted for his prep-school stylishness and also for his obsession with brands. McDonnell's novel *Twelve,* named after a fictional
designer drug, is compared to Bret Easton Ellis's novels as well as
those of the adult nightlife novelists of the 1980s, who wrote when
listing brands was still good for a laugh. "He [McDonnell] is as far
along as Bret was in his craft and his talent," the novelist's editor
tells the *New York Times.*

The cosmopolitan confessionalism of twenty-three-year-old
Molly Jong-Fast has also generated comparisons to the nightlife
novelists—as well as comparisons to her mother, Erica Jong. Jong-
Fast's debut novel, *Normal Girl,* was published and promoted heavily in 2000, when Random House set up Jong-Fast as the poster
child for this new sort of teen writer: "At twenty-one years of age,
she handles her fame with an aplomb that could only come from
years of experience, years of offering sound bytes and photos to the
media under the guise of being the precocious child of famous parents." The book's publicity materials further emphasize her youth,
as well as her celebrity autobiography, noting that "she reminds us
that she is a recent teenager, peppering her conversation with references to *Melrose Place* and rolling her eyes at the mention of a recent

argument with her mother over use of the car." They also underline that the writer is herself a consumerist teen, former drug addict, and a celebu tot: "*Normal Girl* follows Miranda Woke, a seasoned nineteen-year-old New Yorker with a famous set of parents and a well-honed booze and drug addiction, on the road to disaster and then recovery. If it sounds auto-biographical in part, it is."

It makes sense that some of the teen writers are compared with those earlier authors who were so fixated on the branded world. But Ellis, Jay McInerny, and Tama Janowitz prognosticated a synthetic, branded, televisual life. Now we all—and most acutely the teen writers—are trapped in this branded life. Branding youth and seeing the world through an optic of product lines is no joking matter or hipster trope: it's a depressing variety of realism.

CONFESSIONS OF A TEENAGE TEENAGER

Memoirs were once the reward for a famous person who had lived long enough to get around to writing a book. Now they arise out of saleable joy or misery. Anyone can be a memoirist, assuming he or she has a good "coping" story, or simply more moxie than self-consciousness.

Today's teenagers grew up in the period when confessionalism was king. Tarbox took inspiration from Kathryn Harrison's *The Kiss*, a book that tracked Harrison's own taboo-breaking young sexual life (she had a long-term sexual affair with her estranged father). Other teen memoirists also cite the fantasy autobiographies that compose Gotham Girl fiction, works such as *Run Catch Kiss*, *Sex and the City*, and *4 Blondes*, as their forerunners. That means these kids draw on a genre that rests on friends so excessively colorful that they appear day-glo, a first-person narrator in the culture industry (glammy and lovelorn, with unconventional but unassailable good looks), and an endless parade of sexual partners.

Why don't kids aim higher? Maybe because this is a generation that has witnessed the transformation of the writer into a literary brand ("alcoholic famous author's daughter," "sexy incest survivor," "Prozac-swilling 'bitch,'" "postfeminist date-rape denier"). Kids, too, have learned to brand themselves, adopting sobriquets just as digestible as their elders'—"Internet stalker survivor," "strung-out teenage model." Generation Y's writers understand that their budding sexuality and oh-so-personal stories are utterly marketable.

None more so than Benjamin Lebert's *Crazy*, a teen autobiographical novel. Lebert uses the seriousness of his physical condition—he is half-paralyzed to the extent that he can't tie his shoes—to absolve the reader of feeling voyeuristic when reading of the sixteen-year-old's randy meandering. At the onset of the book he introduces himself to his classmates and readers: "Hi folks, my name is Benjamin Lebert. I'm sixteen, and I'm a cripple, just so you know."

After leaving home for the first time to attend an exclusive German boarding school, Lebert loses no time in getting into the raunchy scenes that are his forte. He quickly loses his virginity on a school bathroom floor. He is now ready for the book's crowning moment, when he stands on stage at a strip club running his "hand around Angelique's navel and the ten-mark note follows its every move. Slowly I inch lower. Stick my little finger in her panties." It was this combination of vulnerable exhibitionism and a *Porky's*-goes-to-Munich sensibility that earned the book critical praise, made it a best-seller (its original edition sold 300,000 copies), and eventually launched a popular German movie.

As one of the teen memoirists told me, "I grew up when famous people were also teenagers, like Anna Kournikova or Britney Spears, or they were young people famous for playing teenagers in movies, like Jennifer Love Hewitt." As citizens of the new teen self-branded order, young writers have learned that if you can tell your story, you can sell your story.

PORTRAIT OF THE
AUTHOR AS A YOUNG OLD MAN

Across time, adult writers have striven to replicate the sound of youth, the staccato, impressionistic language of kids. They have tried to imitate their vernacular, immediacy, and passion. Gifted teens who now parade their own early sexual experiences in print are the envy of adult writers who expend so much more effort reaching back into time to re-create their own tender ages and salad days. Rebbecca Ray, who wrote *Pure*, a compelling tale of statutory rape, while she was still a teenager, summarizes the power of the teen writer most engagingly. The reason people are so interested in adolescence, Ray tells me, is that no one can remember what it's really like for very long.

Grown-ups often struggle to achieve a naive wildness that marks the best adolescent memoirists. The authentic-seemingness of the teen memoirs is not lost on adult readers, who have made several of these books best-sellers. They offer the promise of a "real" voice as well as a dose of lascivious nostalgia. It's a wallop of young sex, but from the "right side" of young sex—these are the voices of Lewis Carroll's Alice and Nabokov's Lolita, not the adults who covet them. In *Lolita*, Humbert finds her "a beautiful hardly formed young girl whom modern co-education, juvenile mores, the campfire racket and so forth had utterly and hopelessly depraved," a girl whose precocious, comically refined kiss "of flutter and probe" existed solely for Humbert's amusement and lust. The teen memoirists offer Lolita's tale as if from her own eyes and are likely to be constructing cruel parodies of their sexually predatory elders.

It would be a rare author of any age who could represent sexual desire, or anything, as well as Nabokov. And in their favor, the teen sex memoirists can argue for the sovereignty of their accounts. In anthologies such as 1999's *Ophelia Speaks: Adolescent Girls Write About Their Search for Self,* dozens of teen writers tell of their trials, you feel as if they were catching life *while* they were living it out. (Many of the *Ophelia Speaks* essays deal with some of the struggles of being a teenager in a branded world. One girl writes of her suicide attempt after getting deferred admission to Yale University: "I wanted to kill myself. I tried. A slice, two, three, four, five. Flesh parting cleanly under the fragile, tiny razor blade"; or a friend's eating disorder, "'Isn't she soooo pretty?' Tamara would ask, pointing at the stick-thin model with a Barbie doll body in the Delia*s catalog. 'I'd love to look like her. She's so skinny.'")

Nevertheless, I wonder whether these teens may be too young to realize the lasting implications of creating tell-all and show-all books that occupy an ethically troubling zone. Do they really own their own stories when they tell them and then sell them off when they are so young, before their stories have been revised by experience or memory?

Some would argue that teenage memoirists have taken control of the adult gaze and used it to produce images of themselves for adults to consume. Some would say this is a good thing, preferring the near-child who creates and then manages his image to the grown-up who objectifies children. But that story is too pure in its optimism. In truth, these young writers have absorbed the message that one should publicize one's own life.

But why do kids who are still dependent on their parents and are still in school need to make so much money and make a splash?

If they can't be writers for writing's sake, who can? I take the question to the clever Vizzini. He explains why he wants to be successful as a popular writer rather than a "literary" one.

"I had this moment that I wanted to call my book *The Stranger in My Shoes* and have like an Egon Schiele painting on the cover or something," he says, and then smiles, his shiny brown eyes widening. "But then I realized that for every high-concept, literary novel that succeeds, thousands fail. So I am glad my book is profanity-free and easy to read in a sitting. Look, I was given so much love and respect in high school for appearing in the newspapers. There's incredible social pressure to be famous in my generation. And to make a name for yourself. I wanted to stake my claim. I grew up seeing teen day traders in the 1990s, a television full of teen stars. The ideal age according to the media is fourteen—that's the age of those who fascinate the media and control it." He pauses then smiles again. Winningly, of course.

PART THREE
unbranding

12

Unbranded

"Tell me something about yourself," a Madison Avenue slickster, clad in a shiny gray suit and a pair of Nikes, says. "Is that your natural hair color?"

A teen boy with a wrestler's build answers brightly that he dyes it. "Do you work out?" the adman then asks the kid.

"Of course."

The advertising executive then dismisses the boy. He auditions a young actress, asking her how much she weighs. "A hundred and twenty pounds," she replies. "Way too fat!" her interrogator hoots back.

This routine could well be a real-life visit to a commercial casting agent. It's not, though. It's a scene from a play performed, conceived, and written by students. This one-act is a bit didactic, sure, but it's also funny and knowing, nothing like the over-obvious, gratingly earnest high school theater I can recall. It's also one of the novel tactics kids are using to make sense of, and to fend off, a consumerism that now threatens to engulf them. The actors in this play are part of a passel of teens who resist brand culture in big and small gestures.

Other signs of resistance to branded teenhood: an antischool sponsorship campaign organized by high school students in the late 1990s, wherein kids staged events and printed zines that took aim at everything from Pepsi ads in their high school hallways to Canada's ad-filled Youth News Network. One then-teen, Sarah Church, incited her classmates to testify at her local school board meetings against the branding of her high school, Berkeley High. The other students mocked her as "the girl who hates Pepsi" and were generally "intensely cynical" and brand-obsessed, Sarah recalls. Undaunted by her classmates' derision, Sarah started the center for the now defunct Commercial-Free Public Education's Youth Advisory Board. Board members have continued the fight. In 2000, when one youth advisory member angered his school officials by whipping out a video camera and filming his school's "Cadillac day"—an event where car salesmen hawked six Caddys on school property to kids who were just getting their licenses. He now uses the film as documentary evidence.

Sometimes talking back to sponsored power in this way is a risky proposition. In May 2001, seventeen-year-old Tristan Kading was threatened with suspension from his public high school in Stoningham, Connecticut, when he challenged a McDonald's representative while the rep held "practice interviews" with the school's students in the cafeteria. Tristan accused the visitor of fronting for an exploitative company that lies about what substance its French fries are cooked in—McDonald's infamously said its fries were prepared in vegetable oil, although they had been flavored with beef tallow. Exercising his skills at rhetoric and analysis didn't get Tristan a high grade, though. Rather, he was booted out of his auditorium, where a golden arches flag was flying high, and he landed in the principal's office. Tristan is a handsome blue-eyed kid with short straw-colored hair and a personal affect that could be described as either sullen or shy, clad in Converse sneakers and the typical shabby T-shirt from the Salvation Army, he recalls that his principal told him to write an apology to the McDonald's rep and read it over the PA system or face suspension. Scared, he did so, but he took his revenge afterwards.

Having come of age in the 1990s, Tristan knew that the media can be used to turn the power of the logo against itself. He wrote a letter about the incident to a local newspaper. After a series of meetings, the district reconsidered the job event.

There are nodes of unbranding kids who are less overtly political than Tristan. They shop at thrift-stores, for instance, to demonstrate that corporations have less hold over them than over their peers. They don't identify with any movement in particular, but they'll soon enough tell you that what they dream about isn't represented by anything on offer at the store.

The unaffiliated kids aren't easily identified or counted, but they do represent a real counterbalance to their Tommy T-shirt-clad peers. Lindsay, a seventeen-year-old New Yorker, is one example of a kid who embraces an anticonsumerist ethos, but without subscribing to politics. "I have an esoteric pride in not buying stuff," she explains. She's small and delicately pretty. Her skin is almond-colored, her fine sandy hair bunched in a messy ponytail. Her hazel eyes tend to narrow with a hint of anger. Lindsay reads books about coercive marketing, but then she parties a lot at her friends' apartments around New York City. Wearing thrift store clothes, her cotton shirt torn at the wrists, she goes to her friends' homes and listens to the stylishly frayed Manhattan band The Strokes over and over again. Lindsay describes her parents as being mostly concerned about why she no longer wants to be a doctor.

She represents the outlying areas of a potential backlash: If kids feel they have been excessively manipulated, they may turn away from brands. The teen clothier Delia*s, for instance, included Lindsay in a focus group, she says, to get an "arty" kid's perspective. According to Lindsay, their efforts were a total bust—she claims she was silenced when she said she wasn't familiar with Shakira, a new Latina chanteuse featured in Delia*s latest print advertisement. "It was an insult to my intelligence," she says.

These casual anticonsumerist sentiments don't pass teen marketers by unnoticed. Even at the APK/Golden Marbles marketing fiesta, the marketers recognized that so-called normal teens aspire for something beyond more product and better packaging. "Teens are asking themselves, 'How can I bring "utopia" into my personal life?'" one of the Golden Marblers had said. When I heard it, I wondered what "utopia" could possibly mean to them; surely not a place of perfect laws, governments, conditions, or perfectible human society. I soon understood that to the marketers, "utopianism" is advertising that speaks to the occasional idealism of teens and tweens. Brand managers now concoct ways to stuff teens' loftier desires into packaged goods. "Utopianism," for marketers, is about ensuring that the idealists in the teen crowd are hooked up with teen television shows such as *Buffy the Vampire Slayer, Charmed,* and *Dark Angel*—all of which, the marketers say, speak to teens' needs for "religion and spirituality."

A craftier way that companies try to satisfy teens' errant high-mindedness and altruism is by associating their brands with a good cause, a method termed *cause-based marketing.* According to a 2000 Cone/Roper Cause-Related Teen Survey, 89 percent of teenagers said they would likely switch brands to one associated with a good cause. In 1999, 55 percent said they would switch out of altruism. Companies seemed to take note: Home Depot began supporting Habitat for Humanity, and Target allowed shoppers to name which schools will receive 1 percent of a shoppers' purchases.

Given that teen branding has taken on a patina of charity, it makes sense that unaffiliated kids who dream of a better world are confused about what to buy into and what to resist. There are plenty of divided minds among Generation Y, and they all respond to a lot of mixed messages. One thirteen-year-old, Olive, a beautiful and thoughtful dark-eyed biracial teen who lives in a New York suburb, explains her contradictory feelings about her appearance and the media one day when I pay a visit to her summer camp: "A while ago, we would have been affected by TV, but now we've been taught to not be affected by it. We've been told [by our mothers and teachers], 'Don't look in the magazines. You don't have to look like they are showing you on TV.' It's almost like today, there's trendiness on one side and an antitrend trend on the other."

Living inside this opposition, even the kids who favor what I call "unbranding" wrestle with how much importance they will give the trendiness that defines today's adolescence. One of the actresses in the anticommercial school play flushes when she admits she wears Old Navy clothes; another actor guiltily admits to his love of television commercials.

THEN AGAIN, MAYBE I WON'T

Jon Vine, seventeen, the playwright of the anticorporate theater production, is not confused about which side of the brand divide he dwells within. Jon tends to look for a secret pattern of commodification in life. He likes bearing witness to the ways in which teens are being covertly sullied: "I feel manipulated when the teen films are so emotionally bombastic," he exhorts. I sit with him and the cast in the high school auditorium on an afternoon before a performance. Jon lives in a small town a full two hours north of Kittery,

Maine, and attends Maranacook Community School in Readfield, Maine. The area begins with a necklace of Timberland and North Face outlets at the Maine-New Hampshire border; the outlets lead into the nearby coastal towns where the Bush dynasty summers. There are signs reading "Maine: The Way Life Should Be." There are "game weighing stations," where hunters take their daily dead. There are local convenience stores displaying chalkboards that enumerate how many does and bucks have been killed each month.

The actors in the school play have been urged on by their teacher, Peter Duffy, thirty. Duffy is one of those teachers whose work is full of the same possibilities for devotional self-sacrifice and transcendence as, say, ministry and carpentry. "Everything is about purchasing. We are not allowing them to be kids. In fifth grade suddenly they now have to have 'a look' and 'a behavior,' and there are sexual expectations at that age as well—this is adulthood without the age and the power," says Duffy, as a way of explaining his passion for the students' play.

Jon's a very skinny boy; a pleasant flush of red dusts the tops of his cheeks, his wide-apart eyes are dark blue. "I don't like when films force us with excessive cues on what and how to feel," Jon says. "They think we are kids and we will be told to buy the Gap and we will just do it."

One girl in the cast draws comparisons between the youth of her mother in the 1960s and her own adolescence, perceiving a decay in values. "My mom was a seamstress and had no money and sewed her own clothes," says the freshman actress through a mouthful of braces. "Even wearing her own clothes though, she could still be one of the popular kids. I was a kid till seventh grade," she continues, "but my mom was a kid till she was in eleventh grade. Marketing turns teens into adults."

Jon says that he decided to write a play about the rude power of marketing men and the effects of television's beauty ideals on girls "because we are manipulated by the images of cool, where we kids were taught to despise who we were." Jon's analysis contains something of the age-old ability, desire, and fantasy of adolescents to see through the hypocrisy of the adult world.

The leaders among the coterie of kids who are brand resisting can be aggressive in their detection and rejection of purchasing culture. They might even seem a bit paranoid if the multinationals slithering into their classrooms weren't so omnipresent. Nick Salter, seventeen, did "walk throughs" of his high school, Cherry Creek High School, located in a suburb outside Denver; he noted all the corporate products being pitched to him in his schools hallways and classrooms and reported the results to the now-defunct Center for Commercial-Free Education. By Nick's count, there were thirty-four soda machines, all displaying ads. Ad-plastered billboards circle his school's baseball and football fields. There were textbooks that use M&Ms in their examples. His cafeteria had both Domino's and Blimpie's outlets. The paper covers available for protecting his books were from corporate sponsors as well, companies such as Clinique; part of the free cover is a coupon for the company's powders and blushes. Nick expressed outrage at the stealthy selling tactics; he felt as if he were being duped by an adult world. He started to be aware of it in middle school: "We were made to watch commercials on Channel One in sixth grade," he says. "Something was wrong with that picture."

Tristan, the McDonald's rebel, thinks along the same lines. "I am there to learn school things, not corporate dogma," he says. "I am the kid who wouldn't wear name brand labels, made by slave labor." Like Jon Vine and Nick Salter, Tristan believes that the corporate mask is part of a falsification created by adults to take advantage of him. As adults, we may think of Cadillac salesman coming to school as ludicrous. Unbranding kids, because they are kids, may feel truly outraged. Many of them just recently realized how deeply the commercial world penetrates their lives, and they feel they have spent years being duped.

Politics aside, there is also the bare and universal truism that some kids just don't want to distinguish themselves from their peers and, like teens in other eras, Tristan and Jon and Nick seek to create a distinction between themselves and less discerning adolescents. As Sarah Thornton writes in the 1996 book, *Club Cultures: Music, Media and Subcultural Capital,* young people "construct elaborate scenarios whereby the superficial or belated activities of *other* young people act as a yardstick of the depth and style of their own culture." But the self-presentation of today's teen-brand resisters indicates something else to me. Being anticorporate and unbranded is a much needed "other" identity for kids who have been cast as demographics rather than as citizens. Anticorporate crusader is one of a few possible maverick personae available. When teenagers look for an alternative and an outside to a system where postpunk and street fashion was long ago co-opted, they often come up empty-handed.

Jon and kids like him who understand consciously that they have grown up in the twilight of mass-produced cool are still looking for the flip side of a world of appearances. He understood and was even in awe of the logic of branding and its celebrity glow. Like other unbranded kids, though, he refused to supplicate before powerful brands. Instead, he transformed his worshipping impulse into vitriolic, gleeful rejection. As Naomi Klein writes in the 2000 book *No Logo: Taking Aim at the Brand Bullies,* anticorporate activism borrows the hipness and celebrity from the brands it seeks to critique and ultimately disempower.

"Logos that have been burned into our brains by the finest image campaigns money can buy, and lifted a little closer to the sun by their sponsorship of much-loved cultural events are perpetually bathed in a glow," Klein writes. She calls this effect the "loglo."

Anticorporate activists are "able to enjoy its light," she says, "even as they are in the act of attacking a brand. They draw energy from the power and mass appeal of marketing, at the same time as they hurl the energy right back at the brands that have so successfully colonized our everyday lives."

TOTAL REQUEST DEIOURNEMENT

In New York City's Times Square, a bunch of teen activists are rallying. The war in Afghanistan has just started and this action is a combination of peace activism and what amounts to an anti-MTV action.

Sandra Garcia, sixteen, stands in front of the building where MTV has its headquarters on an unseasonably warm day. She is small and thin, her black eyes adorned with blue glittery eye shadow, her slim torso clad in a Rock Star T shirt. She's trying to attract the roving cameras of *Total Request Live*, Carson Daly's popular hour-long music request program. (*TRL*, a call-in video show, regularly pans down at the teens and tweens as they stand waiting for their moment on the street below). Sandra is certainly wearing clothing that would be most appropriate for sending her love to Carson and every dreadful boy band under the sun, but she is there to mess with the program in the name of peace.

Sandra and maybe twenty other kids formed an ad hoc coalition led by Benjamin Quinto, now twenty-four, and founder of the Global Youth Action Network. The signs they are holding are not the usual *TRL* fodder. They read: "New Yorkers Say No to War, Youth Wants Peace, It's Our Future, Carson." One kid holds an MTV sign with the V inverted and inserted into the upside-down "v" of a peace sign. Meanwhile, Sandra affixes paint to her sign, which reads, "An Eye for an Eye Leaves the Whole World Blind."

"We are in so much pain, why would we want to inflict it on other countries?" says Sandra. "We are brainwashed by TV and brands: MTV and America is trying to overpower other countries. I live in New Jersey and no one agrees with me back home, but people are afraid to know the truth. Look at them screaming for their bands. All their lives revolve around this crap. Look at these MTV kids."

The activists could not have picked a better symbol of America's domination of global youth culture to rally against than MTV. For one thing, since September 11, 2001, the music television channel's high school year abroad version of globalism has received high marks politically; MTV is no longer considered ditsy and avaricious. Now it's patriotic because it stages musical events for the troops and tries to make inroads with youth audiences in the Middle East. For another, even before 9/11, MTV was viewed in over 342 million households in 140 countries, on thirty-one channels and in seventeen languages. Eighty-five percent of global teens who watch MTV, according to a 1996 survey, do so every day. They are thus much more likely than other teens to wear the teen uniform of jeans, running shoes and denim jackets and to respond to brands such as Nike, Sony, and Levi's.

Janet Scardino, former vice president of international marketing at MTV Networks (now senior vice president of international marketing at AOL-Time Warner), did once feel a pang about this indoctrination of a global population with American youth drek, especially in developing nations; she wondered in an interview in 1996 with *American Demographics* whether there might be concerns in some of MTV's foreign markets "that Western media will cause national identity and values to suffer." Scardino ended that interview by reassuring herself that MTV creates no adverse affects in developing countries. "What we've seen is that the media doesn't change values or ethics," she said. "We're seeing a growing communality among global youth as it relates to media habits and spending habits."

Sandra's problem at the moment of the antiwar MTV rally is less the global implications of MTV than the local implications. She gestures contemptuously at the regular *TRL*ers, who are wearing tank tops and baseball caps and T-shirts with Abercrombie logos. "I came out for *TRL* because I watch it every day at home," said *TRL*er Aly Nutter, seventeen. She is also wearing glitter eye shadow. Her sign reads "Alan Is Yummy." "Alan from Lit," Aly says. "You know, the band?" She's from the Midwest, came for the weekend, watches *TRL* everyday: "It keeps my mind off my homework." "We came to be closer to Carson," says a girl, whose name I don't catch, from Leighton, Pennsylvania. Elsewhere: an "I Love Boobs" sign, a Backstreet Boys sign.

The MTV event, like so many of the strategies of the unbranding kids I've spoken to, appears to be of like mind with the anti-advertising magazine *Adbusters*, an exceptionally glossy Canadian publication that instructs its readers in the best tactics for messing with the intrusive hydra head of corporate culture—playful but aggressive subversion. (Another *Adbuster*-ish action: Tristan wearing an Old Navy staff T-shirt into the store, pretending to be a staffer, and warning all shoppers about Old Navy's child exploitation; or sixteen-year-old Sean Merat's celebration of Buy Nothing Day, where he put up Buy Nothing Day posters on his school's walls and "culture jammed" by "selling boxes of nothing and CDs of nothing" and also placing Buy Nothing postcards on top of the ads that ring the interiors of buses.)

The manual for the Adbusters unbranding kids is *Culture Jam: How to Reverse America's Suicidal Consumer Binge—And Why We Must,* written by Kalle Lasn, founder of *Adbusters*. *Culture Jam,* like the MTV rally, and the sensibility of the play in Maine, is one part class clown, one part "detournement," or "turning around," an action that underlines pomposity or falsity (drawing mustaches on an advert femme is a crude example of detournement; a more up-to-date one is the teen with the magic marker who turned an epic sign for a Nike shoe called Presto into the deflating "Not Im-Presto"). Detournement takes its lead from situationism, the anarcho-aesthetic movement that existed from 1957 to 1972. Recent *Adbusters*-endorsed activism has included political art projects through which kids manipulate the logos of McDonald's, Gap, and M&Ms to "undermine corporate credibility"; video games in which the object is to attack logos; and an official "TV turn off" week.

For the *Adbusters* crowd, the anticorporate movement is one outcome of the identity politics of the late 1980s and early 1990s. In *Culture Jam,* Lasn writes that activists have "reconfigured the fragmented forces of identity politics into a new, empowered movement" in response to the observation that "America is no longer a country. It's a multimillion dollar brand. America™ is essentially no different from McDonald's, Marlboro or General Motors. . . . A free authentic life is no longer possible in America™ today."

Those at the MTV peace rally were aspiring for that free, authentic life by using the gleaming aura of the MTV logo itself.

And they are right to do so. After all, MTV is the signifier of the consumerist pop oblivion that has swallowed youth culture. The station proudly trumpets the "360 degree" lifestyle of its audiences. "Our users have televisions, computers and stereos in their rooms, often all on at the same time," Sarah Cohen, vice president of programming and production of MTV.com, told the branding trade magazine, *Brandchannel.*

This is a corporation that has programmed two generations of American kids to buy more, more, more. And so it isn't surprising when the youth politics near the MTV studios is quashed. The

MTV security guys show up and tell the activists to get off the sidewalk and away from *TRL*'s cameras. "You are standing on private property," they tell the protesters. "You have to be carrying signs that have to do with *TRL.*"

The organizer of the protest, a guy in his early twenties, argues with the security guy. But this is a month after September 11, and suddenly policemen are everywhere. When I look up for Sandra, she's gone.

13

DIY Kids

Mishy is not a protestor or a teenage political playwright. Still, at seventeen, Mishy is serious. She has already refused Logo U. culture in a big way: She's not being tutored for the SATs and may never take that standardized test. She puts little stock in attending a designer university, or even in attending university at all. That attitude arose partially because, like an estimated 850,000 American kids (or 1.7 percent of U.S. students from five to seventeen), Mishy opted out of school entirely to attend school at home. She did so when she was in eighth grade, and she left school for the usual reasons kids hate school.

"It was fake and the cliques were bad," says the five-foot-six thin and olive-skinned teen. Her wavy hair is dirty blonde and long and she tends to wear drawstring cargo pants. "The conformity was intense: you had to have the right brand clothing," she explains. "Nike, or Skechers and Doc Martens if you were alternative. You had to shave your armpits and legs when you were thirteen or it was humiliating—everyone else had the coolest clothes, everything shaved, all this makeup."

"Unschooling," a word coined by the late educational theorist John Holt, author of *Teach Your Own,* is what Mishy chose to pursue instead. Unschooling means that Mishy has basically educated herself, making up her own "curriculum" out of bits and bobs of the outside world. The impetus for Holt's neologisms *homeschooling* and *unschooling* arose from his own fervent hatred for traditional schooling. As early as 1969, in the book *The Underachieving School*—in a chapter titled "Schools Are Bad Places for Kids"—Holt asserted that children's natural curiosity is stymied at the school gates. "He learns that in real life you don't do anything unless you are bribed, bullied or conned into doing it, that nothing is worth doing for its own sake," Holt writes. That aversion to traditional school motivates another more recent champion of unschooling, Grace Llewellyn, whose 1997 book *The Teenage Liberation Handbook: How to Quit School and Get a Real Life and Education* describes quitting school as removing "the biggest obstacle" that keeps teens from "flowering," and regarding college she exhorts teens: "Don't enroll just because it's expected of you." (Llewellyn is more misguided, though, when she describes homeschooling and unschooling as elevated practices, Rilkean with contempt for the "bustling social activity" of traditional school, which is merely "shallow and unfulfilling.")

Although the unschooling movement and the larger homeschooling movement have expanded in the last forty years, the exact numbers are harder to estimate because of a scarcity of statistical evidence and the elaborate ruses parents use to get their kids off the radar screens of school officials. The National Center for Education Statistics puts the number of homeschooled kids at 850,000 in 1999, but homeschooling enthusiasts almost double that estimate, counting from 1.5 million to 1.7 million. (Unschooling advocates believe that from 10 to 15 percent of those children are currently being unschooled.)

Although parents often have a large role in their kids' choice to unschool, the kids are usually the ones taking the real risks—with their decision, they immediately put themselves outside of what

Mishy dubs "pop" teen society. Unschooling is the unbranding of school and of adolescent identity—its participants say they no longer feel like "teenagers" or "high school students." It can radicalize kids to the point where they reject conventional labels wholesale.

For instance, few of the unschoolers I spoke with were prepping and pitching themselves in order to enter posh name colleges. "I didn't need college; I could do college better than college could do itself," says Peter Kowalke, an unschooling "graduate" who is now twenty-three and believes that the attitude toward college is a key difference between the unschoolers of his generation and those who opt for the "self-directed" learning of today.

"Unschoolers are increasingly saying, 'We don't need to play the college admissions game,'" Kowalke continues. He has taken a leave from the loosey-goosey, anti-institutional Hampshire College in Amherst, Massachusetts. (Hampshire is a favorite for unschoolers as the school doesn't place much emphasis on letter grades in evaluating applicants and doesn't give letter grades for courses.) "That you have to go to university is societal brainwashing," concludes Kowalke. "Why was I paying so much money for college? If I was to spend that money myself, I could do a lot more with it."

Needless to say, Kowalke's adversarial stance stands in stark contrast to the increasing levels of intensity with which many teens now chase the upper-echelon branded college dream. And the unschooling movement's expansion in an age of elite university mania is not a historical accident. The parents and teachers that choose unschooling tend to speak of it as a response to the commercialization of childhood and adolescence.

Kenneth Danford, cofounder and director of an unschoolers' school-without-walls called North Star Self-Directed Learning for Teens in Western Massachusetts is a man who left public school teaching because of what he derisively calls an "age-appropriate, packaged curriculum." North Star costs a student, or, in unschooling parlance, "a member," $2,500 a year. The school consists of four rooms at the bottom of an unremarkable 1980s red brick office building on Route Nine, the main artery between Northhampton and Amherst. It's a place where kids who wish to teach themselves go to learn about things such as "media literacy" but also to take up apprenticeships and learn skills. Mishy, for instance, set up a photo darkroom at North Star.

Danford, like so many in the unschooling scene, is deeply suspicious of standardized tests, standardized curriculum, and even grades. "It's all on a come-as-you-want basis," Danford says of North Star. "It's not consumer oriented; we don't like grades, logos, brownie points."

Parents also present their decision to unschool as way to protect their kids from consumerism. "I remember when my son was three years old, all the other parents were encouraging their children to play with brand products like Ninja Turtles—I really didn't like the materialism at all," recalls Françoise, whose son Zack, fourteen, is a lifelong unschooler. Zack writes for hours each day, reads Harry Potter books and goes to the Metropolitan Museum of Art in New York. Sometimes he bakes bread, sometimes he gets lessons in medicine from a doctor, one of his parents' friends. I find myself slightly jealous of his bohemian lifestyle, but the life Françoise and Zack have chosen is more than just a daily dose of the demimonde. Zack is a boy of principles. He sees conventional schooling as a regime of faddishness that he has had the luck to avoid.

"If you are in schools, you must love Britney Spears and trendy bands and the right clothes," he says. He has preternaturally poised diction and speaks in full sentences. His voice is musical. "I insist on wearing tight clothes because I don't want to be mistaken for those people who wear loose jeans because they are fashionable. Just because you are a certain age you are expected to be alike."

Mishy and Zack and unschooled teens like them describe themselves as maturing in a singular, liberated way, growing up without boredom. They say, thankfully, that they are free of the grade-grubbing competition that is ever on the rise in mainstream sectors and can ignore the "hot clothes and hot music" that distract and oppress their peers. Mishy, now of college age, is still simply not, she says, "ready to give her life over to the school." When she looks at her brother, an "athlete and a popular high school kid with the right clothing and the right style, I feel like I got away with something." What she has gotten away with, she says, is "never having to ask to go to the bathroom or get a note from my parents to go to a class. I was always a person before I was a teenager."

BASEMENT PARADISE

"I saw the signs advertising decay," sang the band, The Insurgent. "Saw the graveyards on your strip mall street, saw the standards I refuse to meet / I don't want to be dead inside." It was three in the morning. Four members of one band, Sometimes Walking, Sometimes Running, stood in the audience screaming at varying pitches while The Insurgent was singing in an off-key growl. The dancing was messy, thirty-five kids swaying and jumping about. Someone turned out the lights; one band member grabbed a mike and just shouted over the feedback and pounding of the drums. The youth in the audience ranged from slightly plump and bespectacled boys with pale skin, wet with sweat, to skinnier boys with gel in their hair and studs on their clothing. One boy and girl had their first kiss that night, in the dark, while everyone else was watching the band in a nursery-school classroom or dancing between spilled building blocks.

The vexed antimall lyrics and the curious homespun venue might be rough around the edges, but to them it's a glorious little paradise.

These kids are representative of another swathe of unbranded teens, the DIY or do-it-yourself punk teen and just post-teen scene.

The national DIY punk scene—and there is one, though it's invisible even to most kids—is located somewhere between teen political activism and the surly pubescent hardcore music fandom of yore. DIY punk means that kids put on their own shows in their houses or make their own flyers, without the backing of recognizable record labels, and play in shows that center around the building of their youth communities rather than building their band's brand identity. On the face of it, the DIY punks might appear to be another youth culture revival movement.

The DIY punk scene was first animated by teens in the late 1970s. Basements emerged as concert space for fans and performers too young and sometimes too poor to attend shows in bars and clubs (a major band of that period was Minor Threat). Early DIY bands weren't as self-conscious about their down-market autonomy as this new crop of kids, however. Today's DIYers have taken the practice further underground: As often happens, those who follow the earlier generations of a scene and who haven't yet "sold out" are even stricter about their value systems than their predecessors. Some have developed a distinctly anticorporate edge that extends past their distaste for commercial music spaces. They stage "actions" that combine these two elements, as on the occasion in summer 2001 when fifty kids took over a Kinko's copy shop at the Roosevelt Field Mall in Garden City, New York, and put on an illegal concert. Guitarists from Sometimes Walking, Sometimes Running plugged into the copy chain's generator. (That month, they had spent a lot of time with friends who worked at the store making what one band member called "cryptic flyers" for their outfits, and had in the process mapped out Kinko's resources.) They started to play, their songs a wash of feedback and wrathful anti-institutional lyrics—and at that moment the kids felt the neutered mall space had become *theirs*.

The Long Island DIYers have another idea of teen paradise: the bottom of the suburban ranch houses that belong to DIYer families, where fifty sweaty kids, almost all boys, scream and intone. In the words of one DIYer, "We wanted to reject the continual cycle of consumption by creating self-sufficient alternative spaces."

I found the Long Island branch of the DIY teen scene through Ben Holtzman, now a twenty-one-year-old student at Vassar College. Holtzman had just completed a digital documentary film, *Between Resistance and Community: The Long Island Do It Yourself Punk Scene*, which he began when he was nineteen. He has been a DIYer since he was sixteen. The film, which Holtzman worked on with two friends, resembles the DIY scene itself. It's a rough-hewn and immediate portrait of kids trying to find meaning and solidarity through a punk scene of their own making. They are modern-day Lost Boys who range from cute spike-haired bleached blonds to shlubbier shy kids to vitriolic "rebels."

Holtzman, like most of the Long Island DIYers, grew up in a different sort of community than the punk one he made. His was an average family—white, wealthy, and "broken," his mom an understanding social worker and his dad a less understanding attorney. Holtzman was a kid whose hero was Donald Trump (he wanted to be Trump's penpal). Until seventh grade, that is, when he discovered punk, a movement that was already almost twenty years old. He found DIY three years later, when he picked up a flyer for a do-it-yourself punk gig and checked it out. Soon, he was going to shows once a week and found the routine "comforting, a thousand times better than high school. They talked about issues that I thought were important." Holtzman had uncovered a solution to the alienation he had felt in high school, where he didn't drink (few in the

DIY scene do) and wasn't of the same mind as the popular kids "who wear Abercrombie and the Gap and whose social life revolves around shopping and hooking up with each other." Holtzman was gay and was uncomfortable about coming out in high school. But in the DIY scene—in sharp contrast to the often homophobic hardcore scene—Holtzman felt safe. "We decided we were going to create our own space where money and spending wasn't necessary; we were sick of what we were seeing on the outside," he says.

"As a teen you are only the money that you can spend," continues Holtzman, his voice level but insistent. "Who you are is going to be assumed from the T-shirt you are going to buy, but there's no real connection between you and the T-shirt. I mean, my friends didn't make the products that were supposed to be defining me, they were made in sweat shops."

According to the Long Island DIYers, the scene has taken on a new intensity over the last five years. It has a longer history than this, of course: The current DIY punk scene is an offshoot of the first wave of punk that started in the mid-1970s. The DIYers of that era of punk had a similar desire to expose the false consciousness of workaday existence. As Greil Marcus writes of the Sex Pistols in *Lipstick Traces: A Secret History of the Twentieth Century*, "Damning God and the state, work and leisure, home and family, sex and play, the audience and itself, the music briefly made it possible to experience all those things as if they were not natural facts but ideological constructs."

If DIY gained currency during the punk-and-xerox-mad 1970s, it took an increasingly activist emphasis in the 1990s, according to George McKay's *DIY Culture: The Politics of Party and Protest in Late Nineties Britain*. The Long Island DIYers were inspired by. Reclaim the Streets, an anticar group composed of teens as well as adults who blocked off roads and highways and then staged street parties, thousands of celebrants in attendance. McKay considers these Reclaim the Streets events to be more than just bacchanalias; rather, they combine "social criticism" with "cultural creativity in what's both a utopian gesture and a practical display of resistance."

Of course, the actions and basement performances of the Long Island DIYers are not just acts of political resistance. They are also a stylized (and sometimes a self-conscious) form of teen social behavior that has existed for decades, if not centuries. Kids have long tended to float to edges of cities and towns to hang out. They voyage to median strips, piers, parking lots, and hillsides, and they skate and surf, all to avoid the controlling gaze of the adult world. Teens in the twenty-first century with the public spaces available to them increasingly diminished and deteriorated, must work harder to find so-called cool places. This paucity of place and opportunity for kids to hang out thwarts today's teens' ability to develop enclaves, and also to build their identities away from their families' home lives. (The phenomenon is so pronounced that urban geographers study it as a social problem.)

For teens to resist the incursions of the commercial world, they must increasingly take over spaces that are private or public in a limited sense. The British DIYers reclaimed the motorway and the Long Island kids appropriated the mall and the rec room.

Of course, the limitation of the DIYers is their tendency to *stay* in the basement, cultivating their inward-lookingness. Many are content to be part of a clique that refuses norms privately but has little impact in the larger world. Stephen Duncombe, who writes about the American DIY zine scene of 1990's, argues that the danger of these youthful denunciations of the social order is that they happen only on one cultural plane. They don't necessarily have wider effects. Anger that might be expressed in political action or in underground cultural production is sublimated into mere fashionable tribalism.

Indeed, the DIYers are typically quite insular. Holtzman acknowledges the limits of "staying in the basement and hoping the right people are going to find you." He has tried to break out of that trap by "flyering," or giving out Xeroxed copies of invites to shows to a breed of kids he calls "mall punks." Holtzman defines mall punks as those "who shop at the store Hot Topic," a teen clothing chain. In a clear testament to the commodification of punk in general, Hot Topic sells T-shirts for bigger punk bands such as The Clash and The Misfits and the club CBGB. The mall punks, as Holtzman describes them, "hang out at the shopping center all day and sneer at people." The DIY punk scene generally tends to treat these "impure" rebels with disdain bordering on snobbishness.

Still, up close, the DIY punk scene can seem an effective strategy for resisting branded culture. The Long Island kids have made their own family, replete with their version of family values: they share food, music, and expression. At Mikki Vargas's house (she's Mrs. V. or Mama Vargas to the DIYers), the Vargas family hosted fifty or so noisy adolescents and just post-teens in 2001 on many weekends. They would play music in the basement. The room was so hot the windows would steam up and had to stay shut so the neighbors wouldn't complain about the racket. Afterwards, the DIYers ate beans and rice in the kitchen of the modest home that Mama Vargas and her husband, a pastor, share with their eight children.

Vargas, the mother of three of the DIYers, views her sons' scene as all about trying to create an identity and a youth community in a branded suburb. Many of the DIYers are much richer than her own boys and come from somewhat conservative families. Vargas sees these kids' involvement in DIY as a half-rebellion from their parents' values, as well as values of the larger community, of which she describes the "regular" teens as sometimes being spoiled-unto-self-destruction. In a recent incident in her township, two teens who were drag racing a BMW and Corvette accidentally killed a young couple.

Vargas contrasts such corruption with the minimalist, care-based system of the DIYers: "The DIY movement is a lot about self-sufficiency," she says. "They even cut each other's hair." (Vargas's family intersects with the other unbranding retinue discussed in this chapter—all eight of the children were homeschooled.)

One of the cool things that happened at the Vargas DIY shows that doesn't happen at regular live music performances is that members of the audience grabbed the band's mikes and guitars and play after the billed band finishes. This in itself is somewhat subversive in an adolescence now governed by MTV and marked by a severe dividing line between star and fan. The DIY kids work to create performances where neither "star" nor "fan" exists.

Justin Sullivan, the drummer for The Insurgent, tells me about a recent concert where his band decamped from the stage on which they were meant to play and went downstairs, trailing long extension cords, to play in a narrow hallway. The aim, says Justin, was to keep it "intimate, where people are aware of other people. It's the only way to combat the mentality where people go to supposedly 'underground' shows the way they go to the mall. It's a problem to depend on shirts, patches, and pins in order to demonstrate that if you can just own these things and you'll be okay. Being a consumer is so ingrained that people take it underground."

Clearly, there's a purism to the Long Island DIYers. They are wary not only of making T-shirts and badges for their bands but also of charging money for their shows, and even playing for people that they don't, in the words of one DIYer, have an affinity for. (Though it must be said that in the process of trying to protect their identities from brands they create a series of labels for themselves—hard core, thrasher, punk—that resembles the language of brands.)

Part of the conviction the DIYers have about their own authenticity comes from their reliance on live performances and also on their collective memory of these basement shows. Memory is one of the invisible powers of live performance—it gives live shows their romantic aura—and the collective memory of these kids is the wool with which they weave the net of their community.

Unfortunately, this community tends to have an expiration date. The DIYers' intense involvement usually ends by the time they reach their later twenties—one young man still enmeshed in the scene in his twenties complains that there are few models for him of people in their thirties. But for now, the Long Island DIYers I met remain firm in their convictions.

"Our band is not a small capitalist venture, it's not about getting on MTV," says Justin. "It's a place to come together." Justin is one piece of a small but vocal group of kids who won't have their social desires channeled into branded talismans. They may be cast aside by the teen-oriented companies, but never completely. Their example suggests that kids actually do have a buying threshold: Imagine the dark day for marketers when kids look for things that are neither bought nor sold.

14

Schools for Sale

In the middle of December 2001, more than 2,500 teenagers walked out of their Philadelphia public high school classrooms and onto the city's intersections. A rag-tag gang of teens passed hundreds of handsome brownstones in the "city of houses"—also the same time city of poverty. There were five hundred students from the relatively poor Strawberry Mansion High School. There was also a sizeable contingent from swankier magnet schools such as Masterman High School and Central High School. Kids from fifteen schools met in the big plaza of the city hall, a crowd that eventually marched up Broad Street, one of the major thoroughfares. They packed the two-lane boulevard that runs from North to South Philly, passing under the pointy arches of the Victorian Gothic Pennsylvania Academy of Fine Arts and glass office buildings, walking a full half mile until they reached their destination, the state office.

These kids were not slackers looking for a way to cut class. They were activists committed to defeating the privatization of their schools by Edison Schools Inc., a publicly traded, New York–based company that operates more than 133 public schools in twenty-two states and Washington, D.C.

215

They partially succeeded. In the fall of 2001, Mark Schweiker, the governor of Pennsylvania, had proposed contracting the management of the entire public school system's central administration to Edison, along with the operation of up to sixty schools. On April 17, a state panel voted to give only twenty city schools to Edison. The entire district was not turned over, only some contracts; in addition to the Edison-run schools, twenty-five are to be run by two universities, Temple University and the University of Pennsylvania, and a range of smaller for-profit companies such as Chancellor Beacon Academies Inc. and Victory Schools Inc. As the panel conducted its deliberations, the student activists were rallying around the building. Few in the media picked up on the critical role played by the students; their part has been overshadowed by stories about the Edison's sliding stock price and desperate (though finally successful) quest for a new infusion of funds.

At first, neither the diminished role of Edison nor the protracted battle between the school privatization forces and the high school students seemed likely. At that point, city community groups and parents were supportive of the governor's idea that Edison manage the seventh-largest school district in the country. They imagined Edison might be able to create charter-school-like entities, but with more muscle and more fixed curriculum than the typical charter; indeed, the plan seemed to be a potentially expedient way of improving an ailing district in which some textbooks are so old they inform students that one day "man will walk on the Moon." But the faith started to fade in August, after Edison was given $2.7 million to produce a report on the state of the city's educational system. According to its critics, the report tacitly made the case for Edison's own management. Using the SAT, a test not typically invoked as a yardstick of the success of urban school districts, Edison claimed the schools had simply been mismanaged and didn't even mention the role of underfunding and urban divestment in creating the system's ills.

The evidence of underfunding is hard to ignore. For example, according to the *Philadelphia Inquirer*'s yearly survey of area schools, instructional spending per student in Philly for the year 2001 was $4,747. In contrast, in the Mainline suburb of Radnor, instructional spending per student was $9,120. As for teachers' salaries, Philadelphia's teachers topped out at $62,600, and Radnor paid as much as $79,371. Most stark, given that so many Philadelphia students are poor and have limited access to computers and books outside of school, is the 2001 student-to-computer ratio: six-to-one in Philly and three-to-one in Radnor.

Of course, in its own estimation, Edison does a fantastic job. "Students are gaining more than 5 percentiles per year on nationally normed tests and 7 percentage points on criterion-referenced tests," reads the Edison Web site. "Achievement gains have improved while Edison schools have enrolled a higher percentage of economically disadvantaged students—now 70 percent, up from 65 percent last year." But the company's cheery confidence worked against it in Philadelphia. Many Philadelphians felt insulted by the out-of-town educators, who continually derogated local children's scholastic performances in an effort to prove Edison's indispensability. Parents also detected an alliance of state and corporate power against city dwellers, a familiar dynamic in Pennsylvania. School teachers voiced worry about whether they would be able to keep their contracts after privatization (it turned out that the contracts would remain in force); teachers also worried about whether an Edison curriculum handed down from corporate headquarters would be too one-size-fits-all to serve all students well. School employees and their labor unions, faced with job losses as a result of the privatization, also rallied to the cause.

The case against Edison revolved in part around the sometimes spotty scholastic record of Edison schools in Baltimore and other cities, and in part on a larger question; namely, whether a large chunk of a public school system should be run by a for-profit company, especially in a historical moment marked by an uncertain stock market and massive corporate imbroglios. A local journalist went so far to dub the messy takeover plans "Edron," a jibe that would take on more of the air of truth when Edison became the subject of an SEC investigation regarding its improper accounting and classification of revenue. Then in May, a group of angry Edison Schools Inc. investors filed a class action suit against the company, claiming that Edison had painted a misleadingly rosy picture of its business performance. (The result of the SEC inquiry was Edison restating its revenues.)

Once it had lost its momentum, Edison found itself on the defensive. Its most powerful opponents were and continue to be those most affected by it, the students. "The students have provided the spark for opposition," says Paul Socolar, editor of *Philadelphia Public School Notebook*, a quarterly newspaper about the Philly schools. "The student actions have been the most visible and the loudest and have had a real consistency."

The public high school students who continue to oppose Edison do so on two main grounds. First, they see Edison as part of the larger corporate culture that considers young people, and young people of color in particular, just a demographic to be profited from. Second, they see Edison, with its metal detectors and security guards, as the final stage of the increased policing of students.

"I don't have a price tag and my education shouldn't be for profit," says student activist leader Day Augustine, seventeen, who attends West Philadelphia High School. "Do I want to learn that one plus one equals Pepsi?" he added. "Students are not property."

A STUDENT UNION

In February 2002, fifty teen activists gather at the headquarters of the Philadelphia Student Union, a local nonprofit group devoted to school reform and youth activism. The teen members sit on chairs or on the floor near emptied pizza boxes and discus further student responses to the threat of school privatization. The activists demographically and to some extent socially divide into two camps, arty white teens in fingerless arm-length gloves made from cut-up sleeves of shirts and more conservatively dressed African American kids, hair dyed the occasional shade of blonde. A male teen activist arrives with his toddler son and sits next to a female activist just a few years younger but who exhibits a much more teenager-like mien: multiple piercings and a belt made from a radial tire. One girl gives her friend a new set of cornrows, another girl gives a boy a friendly massage.

"Why are schools being privatized?" Eric Braxton, twenty-six, one of the Student Union's two adult organizers, asked the group. It was the fifth month of discussions about Edison and privatization. With his earring and striped shirt, Braxton looks like an honorary teenager. Indeed, he became a member of the union when he was a senior in a Philly high school himself.

Hands shoot up.

"They are trying to set up a franchise," says one teen. "Education as a franchise, like Burger King."

"Because they are preparing us for prison," another boy jokes. The kids laugh, but also look uncomfortable. The students often compare public schools and prisons, the fear in their voices mixing with bravado. In conversation, they extend the prison metaphor to the Edison schools by imagining Edison classes taught from mass-produced scripts, with Edison teachers responsible to a home office; and hallways, like highways, divided by yellow lines down which identically dressed students would have to walk with their hands behind their backs.

(Students do wear uniforms at some Edison schools, and in some schools they are required to walk in single file in the hallways. According to Edison, school uniforms and walks are instituted on a school-by-school basis and not as a blanket policy. Both exist not to police students, according to Edison, but to promote "core values" such as respect and order.)

The students then write a series of recommendations to send to the district to improve schools. More computers, writes Ashley. Involving kids and teachers in the voting process about what to do about privatization, writes Ebony. One activist, Jacob Winterstein, a fifteen-year-old, speaks angrily of "cookie cutter" education and the "falseness" of Edison.

"This is happening in Philly, not in Ardmore [a wealthy suburb of the city], because we are a poor and minority community," Jacob says. As so many of the student opponents of Edison do, Jacob cites the low funding of Philadelphia schools and its disparity with that of schools in suburban districts as the major reason for the public schools' malfunctions. Opponents of Edison believe the schools would be no more likely to succeed in private hands than they have under the auspices of the city and state.

Edison's corporate identity rankles the students greatly as well—they simply don't want to go to a branded "Edison school." Edison's CEO, Chris Whittle, founder of Channel One, the advertising-laden high school television station that broadcasts to 12,000 classrooms a day, and the activists mock Whittle's stuffy bow tie and rail against the specter of Wall Street investors profiting from their education.

"Edison is like Channel One," says Max Goodman, seventeen, a rosy-faced senior. "It will have an unconscious affect on all the students just like advertising in the schools. And the Gap has money into Edison, so maybe one day they'll say, 'This lesson is brought to you by the Gap.'" Max compares Edison to other corporate investors in her school, whose leverage over student behavior she finds troubling. "When we hold bake sales for fund-raisers, our principal tells us we couldn't serve juice or hot chocolate because those drinks compete with the soda brand in our school's beverage machines, Coca-Cola," says Max, rolling her eyes.

"The branding of the schools is not going to make people who get ahead," adds Jacob. "It turns us into a bunch of groundlings. We want proper funding for public school, rather than bringing in a for-profit organization." For Jacob and many of the others, the battle against Edison is the first political movement of their lives. And in the course of the fight, they have used their teen sensibility to put their message across. For example, they turned Sean "P. Diddy" Combs's profit-motivated tune "Bad Boy for Life" into the antiprivatization chant "Y'All Ain't Coming in Here, We Can't Be Stopped Here—Coz It's Students for Life." They ate pizza and held a sleep-out on the steps of city hall. Like the other youth actions against corporatization in this millennial period, the anti-Edison groups are local and draw on support from activist adults in their community.

As with students in other youth movements, these students have also joined up with the larger anticorporate movement. They have also brought together two elements of student activism. In addition, there's a somewhat hackneyed analysis of the identity of the kids taking part in student activisms that the Edison kids were flying in the face of—that white kids tend to concentrate on anticorporate issues, but teens of color are more tuned into their rights in their schools. Clearly, the Edison battle brought both of these activist constituencies together.

That very day in January, the anti-Edison teens were planning a march with Spiral Q Puppet Theater, a Philadelphia-based band of political puppetmakers who participated memorably in puppet-waving actions against the Republican National Convention in the summer of 2000. Together, the teens and the puppetistas planned to build images of Chris Whittle out of papier-mâché. The presence of Spiral Q is one of the many ways the Edison struggle is akin to the anticorporate movement elsewhere—the students and teens at the WTO rallies or campaigning in front of Niketowns in the late 1990s. The kids in Philly also use anarchic and playful methods.

But the pithiest expression of the movement is on the blue stickers pasted on backpacks. You see them everywhere in Philadelphia: "I AM NOT FOR SALE: SAY NO TO PRIVATIZATION," they say. The students can claim only a partial victory in their schools, but it is a victory nevertheless. They have managed to considerably diminish Edison's role in their future.

"We want all the real cliché things—smaller class sizes, to feel part of the schools, to be part of the decision making," Jacob says. "The way the world is set up not everyone can be doctors and lawyers but now they decide for you before you get to kindergarten. All we want is for us all to have an equal chance." Jacob's intensity, like that of the other anti-Edison students, derives from feeling cheated by invisible interests: by adults with lots more money and power than he has.

When I was a teenager in the late 1980s, teen activists directed their energies to the battle to end apartheid and in honor of abstractions like world peace. There was less of the fighting for teens' own rights, against commodification. Now, the youth movement is very much directed at issues of youth and against the forces that oppress them in their schools and at home. Kids may well consider youth itself something of an embattled minority—and that in turn informs their politics, the area of focus being the retention of civil rights in their classrooms. In his *Scapegoat Generation: America's War on Adolescents* and *Framing Youth: Ten Myths About the Next Generation*, Mike A. Males believes that the criminalization of youth intensified during the Clinton administration as part of the Clintonian postpartisan, apologist modus operandi.

"Pounding on the younger generation brings all political stripes together," Males writes, citing the rise in adult sentencings for juvenile criminal offenders (and some death penalties), teen curfews in California, and a broad media demonization of contemporary adolescents for their violence and supposedly rampant sexuality. What's more, Males says, antiyouth rhetoric is merely a mask for racist and classist sentiments. When powerful adults complain about kids, they are really complaining, in an acceptable way, about poor and nonwhite kids and ignoring that race means how present "nonracist" antiyouth policies fill prisons with young nonwhite men.

Eric Braxton says he sees the anti-Edison struggle as part of the struggle against this view of teenagers, particularly black teenagers, as a force to be feared and controlled. Black teens are often characterized as violent "combat consumers," exactly the right kinds of kids for franchise schools because they require discipline and because they will fall for these schools' slick, name-brand surfaces. That African American kids in particular ruthlessly covet brand names has great currency in this country. Anthropologist Elizabeth Chin examined the stereotype in *Purchasing Power: Black Kids and American Consumer Culture* and found "popular media images of crazed and brand-addicted 'inner city' youth willing to kill for the items they want." This bloodthirsty spending and stealing, or "boosting," was not borne out by the black kids Chin studied. The real damage Chin perceived is that the kids have internalized the media image of themselves as consumer predators, part of a "nation of thieves."

The anti-Edison kids are not unworldly brand purists—they wear Puma, Adidas, and Ralph Lauren. But they know the difference between hype and advertising. "They are aware of the whole initiative of corporate America to make money off of low-income people, and they are angry that they are getting the short end of the stick," Braxton says. Clearly, the anti-Edison movement reveals that there are certain things the supposedly brand-addicted teen won't buy into.

The thousands of kids involved in the Edison struggle feel on some level that the world has always thought of them as a demographic for Pokemon or Nike on one hand, and as hooligans who need to be made to walk in straight lines on the other. The Philly activists are more evidence that some among Generation Y have not taken the merchandising of their minds, bodies, and subjectivities lightly. They are willing to fight back.

Afterword

I finished writing *Branded* in the summer of 2002. Since then, the garish, amusing, and often disturbing world of teen and tween marketing has taken some sharp turns for the better—and some for the worse. One unexpected and happy development came in July 2003, when Kraft Foods announced that it would withdraw its advertisements for processed foods from the in-school television station Channel One, caving in to perceived consumer pressure (and also the potential threat of law suits). That same month, Cheerios swore off school sponsorship. Then, finally, New York City's Education Department banned soda and candy from the vending machines of its public schools. The department's action came on the heels of similar measures by school districts in San Francisco and Los Angeles. School districts in Seattle and Nashville have already limited corporate advertising on school signs and banned Channel One, respectively.

But also in 2003, the increased public awareness of in-school corporate practices and corporate and schools' positive actions were being countered by new more nuanced marketing strategies. By September 2003, the New York City in-school ban on sodas and sweets revealed itself to be something of a sham when these soda machines were slated to be replaced with machines full of Snapple beverages. Snapple was now the official brand of the New York City school system, with the promise that it would sell only its branded water and "pure" fruit juices. The company paid $8 million a year for five years for that honor, and for the right to line New York public school hallways with Snapple machines.

Why do teens and children continue to be such an appealing market to companies like Snapple, even for its plain water and juice products? Part of the answer is simple. A bruised economy and caving consumer confidence made the latest swell of teen spending—an estimated $170 billion in 2002 –desperately attractive. The other part is more far-sighted: companies will go to great lengths to develop cradle-to-grave brand loyalty.

Since *Branded* was published, I have also encountered more, and ever more ingenious—or sneaky—techniques for appealing to the teen market outside of the schools. There's advergaming, for instance, a neologism that, like the term "e-waste," may sound even more creepy than it actually is. Never heard of advergaming? A combination of advertisement and gaming, the word translates to using video games to sell hip-hop products, pitching the music to kids as they play on their consoles so that they will be literally programmed to buy it at The Wiz.

For the little ones, there are M & M counting books and Hershey Kisses books to instruct in addition and subtraction. The Dr. Pepper company hired 18-year-olds to write Weblogs that extol a milk-based beverage called Raging Cow. In 2003, the giant Hummer H2 car's manufacturer, General Motors Corp., reached out to first-time car buyers on TV by buying airtime in the 2003 music video for the rapper Ms. Jade's "Ching, Ching" for $300,000. The same year, young adult novels carried the logo Roxy, a surfwear company, and the characters in the novels were meant to be based on the logo's idealized surfer girls: the tween books serve as covert advertisements for beach girl garb and gear.

The British company French Connection launched two raunchy new teen perfumes in the U.S. called FCUK Her and FCUK Him, supported by a $10-million 2004 marketing campaign. The company's so-called Scent to Bed campaign came replete with License to FCUK cards. And text messaging and cross-branded product placement also got its hooks into the teen and tween market in 2003 through the television show "American Idol." In one episode, the show's host held up a Nokia 3650, reminding voters to call in their votes for a favorite star using AT&T Wireless' text messaging service. But the inventive new strategies don't stop there. The Field Trip Factory, a national for-profit organization based in Chicago, sent children to visit sports stores, supermarkets and pet shops during school hours, tours where return shopping trips with their parents were clearly part of the plan.

These emerging strategies require even higher levels of awareness among us if we are to combat their effects, most serious among them being youth obesity.

According to the latest CDC report, 15 percent of teenagers in America are now overweight. On the other end of "the ecology" of body dysmorphia and confused consumption, in 2002, nationwide, 13.5 percent of students had gone without eating for more than a day to lose weight, while 9.2 percent of students nationwide had taken diet pills, powders, or liquids to lose weight. And while some strides have been made by parents' groups to reduce fast-food school sponsorships, the national concern about the effects hasn't led to the wide-scale crackdown that's needed: 10 percent of schools nationwide still have exclusive soda-pouring contracts; 83.5 percent of junior high schools sell soda and 72 percent of high schools sell chocolate bars, while 35 percent of schools that stock brand-name sodas also feature advertising material in school hallways.

Of course, companies' love for teens and tweens is not unrequited: often, teens love the companies back by freely participating in so-called "guerilla" marketing efforts. Since completing *Branded*, I continue to meet teenagers who are so enamored of teen-oriented companies and their products that they willingly work for them for free. I met teen Street Teamers, kids who work unpaid to promote rock bands, sodas, and even PETA to their peers (in the U.K., Street Teamers even promote cigarettes).

Talking with them, I realized that there were aspects of the Street Team phenomenon that I hadn't fully explored. It's a largely invisible workforce with perhaps 100,000 young people who do PR for music, soda, and even PETA for free, at school, in chat rooms, and even at home by sending letters to magazines. An adult Street Team promoter put it this way: these kids don't just want to be part of the band, they want to be part of the label. They want to be insiders, not just of stardom but of the system that helped to create these stars. But in doing so, these kids are exposed not only to the star-making machinery but to unpaid labor, sometimes requiring illegal actions, like putting posters on poles and at bus stations and stickers on public walls.

Since *Branded*'s publication in 2003, I have met numerous teenagers. What I sensed most strongly in my encounters with them was their wish to have their thoughts and feelings regarding the marketplace atmosphere that many of them live in to be heard. There was a working class teen who told me how she felt compelled to go into debt to buy a costly car and insurance in order to keep up appearances in her middle-class high school and the plump teen who complained that today's revealing and undersized teen fashions have made finding "young" clothing impossible. When I asked hundreds of teens about sponsorship in their schools, half were highly conscious of it in their own schools. Some said it didn't bother them but others copped to being irritated and even upset with the level of "compulsory advertising" in their classrooms, study halls, and lunchrooms.

Their examples were startling: being coerced by school administrators to drink the "school soda"; lunchrooms papered with film advertisements and potato chip advertisements; and in one case, a school official who wouldn't listen to a student voice his complaints about Channel One viewing (and who didn't require notice to parents that their kids were viewing Channel One in the classroom.) Many of the teens had seen the school book covers featuring branding by Swedish Fish, Clinique, or Dr. Pepper and, although these books were give-aways, felt the subtle pressure to cover their books with what are ostensibly walking advertisements.

Since *Branded*'s publication, I've also been asked for antidotes to this dilemma from everyone from teenagers to fellow reporters. As a journalist and not a policy maker, I can't pretend to have the best answers. All I have to offer are notions and half measures that can only begin to staunch the excesses of contemporary marketing to children and teens and the troubles they bring.

For starters, corporations that tie their growth and profit goals to the teen market could begin to make voluntary changes of their own. The Canadian Marketing Association has the Canadian Code of Ethics & Standards of Practice, which contains such pleasant guidelines as: "Marketers should exercise caution that they do not take advantage of or exploit teenagers...Marketers shall not use or collect household or personal information from teenagers as a means to gain entry into that teenager's household. Marketers shall not solicit information about a third party from a teenager." Although these guidelines are mere corporate voluntarism and probably treated with a grain of salt, at least they gesture toward awareness and toward limits.

And in Quebec, all advertising to children under the age of 13 is prohibited under the Quebec Consumer Protection Act. Canadian ads directed at children under 12 follow voluntary guidelines under the Broadcast Code for Advertising to Children. Why don't we have such voluntary guidelines in the United States? And why shouldn't video game companies that market violent and logo-ridden games to kids give some of their proceeds to media literacy foundations, a corporate tithe that would go some way toward supporting their claims that they don't exploit their underage gamers? If there's a Net Nanny device for screening prurient content for minors, why shouldn't their be a Corporate Nanny preventing minors from being solicited on-line by spam or bots or even chat-room Street Teamers shilling for Jones Cola, and preventing data capture of minors' personal information?

The corporate side, of course, always makes mention of the role of parents in the equation: Isn't it their job to monitor their children's spending habits, to prevent them from credit card use and debt, to keep them from wasting hours of their weeks working for a cola company as an unpaid sales person? Certainly parents (and by parents I mean guardians, aunts, caretakers, grandparents et cetera) must also play an active role, as they have in the schools, if anything is to change. But given that commercial ideology and practices work differently than they did in the past, when commercial messages were more often limited to such obvious, bounded strategies such as print advertisements and billboards, new lessons in media literacy lessons are needed. Just as parents are encouraged to have open discussions with their children about sex, drugs, and school, they could also have discussions about a hyper-marketed culture that manufactures so many unaffordable desires.

Although teen marketers, the teen-oriented companies, and the strapped schools selling naming rights to companies did not create the problem of status consciousness or the ensuing taunting and bullying between kids, they have helped to ensure that today's coin of the realm in middle schools are superfluous clothes and quickly obsolescent gadgets. While fashion, self-adornment and material culture are often fantastic, expressive outlets in themselves, when they are excessively costly, hard-sold and so totalizing that they occlude minors' other forms of self-hood, they emerge as problems.

Perhaps parents can start by asking themselves, and their children, simple questions. How does it feel to grow up in an atmosphere where an eight-year-old boy gets teased for being poor by his friends for not owning a Play Station? How does it feel to be a teen girl who doesn't eat lunch on weekends in order to save money for clothes, while her friends jump turnstiles and steal credit cards in order to save or boost enough money for the full autumn line of FuBu? There are many more examples of such difficulties—and the difficulties cannot be laid solely at the feet of the marketers. Families and community groups are going to have to engage in complicated conversations as well, in which the adult himself may well be no beau ideal.

These conversations are difficult because merely teaching tweens how to "read" advertisements isn't enough anymore. Today, we all read articles that are advertisements and advertisements that resemble articles and, as surveys show, kids have trouble keeping the two separate. It's not clear that that difference is always obvious to adults either. Subtler lessons are now necessary in how to tell an editorial piece from catalogue copy and vice versa.

Grassroots efforts by parents and advocates, appealing to fears for the public health of young people, have been highly effective. As with the anti-tobacco campaign in earlier decades, changes in social life often start with small-scale campaigns that circulate around public health and then broaden out. In the next five years, parents and educators could work for further bans on book-cover advertisements and advertising posters in the hallways. There might finally be a ban on schools giving their naming rights to companies. Parents who think selling candy bars and sodas at school is a problem can likely agree that kids identifying their schools with a supermarket chain or a paint company isn't so healthy either. And perhaps kids and teens will once again be able to run around gymnasiums that are named, rather quaintly, after human beings.

Index